Introduction

"Christmas in Arizona doesn't ever seem just right," one of my neighbors in Tucson groused one December afternoon as the sun beat down upon us.

His comment took me aback and then I realized he was thinking of the "back east" Christmases of his youth, replete with snow drifts, sleigh bells, and carolers wrapped in woolen mufflers.

To me, Christmas in Arizona is the image of the grizzled old prospector with his laden burro standing in front of the Superstition Mountains. It is saguaro cactus strung with twinkling colored lights or draped with red Santa Claus caps with their downy white tassels.

Christmas in Arizona is carolers in scarlet colored shorts with white tee shirts emblazoned with "Happy Holidays." It's tumbleweed snowmen, incense burning in miniature tee-pees, and roadrunner decorations hanging from live evergreen trees.

Christmas in Arizona is that rare but sensationally beautiful snowfall in the desert, the Indian dancers on the rim of the Grand Canyon, and the proud crimson-feathered cardinal singing to me from the branch of an oleander bush.

Christmas in Arizona is the myriad of holiday plants that grow in the state—lush bougainvillea, poinsettia, mistletoe and the red-berried pyracantha.

Christmas in Arizona is the fresh grapefruit, lemons, oranges, dates, and figs that grow here. It is the holiday meal served on a patio complete with green corn tamales, turkey enchiladas and pecan pie.

Christmas in Arizona is a land full of color and contrast. It is the desert plants, the decorated city streets and the majestic mountains. In short, Christmas in Arizona is simply a magical, mystical and magnificent experience!

v

Christmas

in

Arizona

Recipes, Traditions and Folklore
for the Holiday Season

by

Lynn Nusom

GOLDEN WEST ☼ PUBLISHERS

Cover Photograph by Dick Dietrich

Also by Lynn Nusom:

> *Christmas in New Mexico Cook Book*
> *New Mexico Cook Book*
> *The Tequila Cook Book*

Library of Congress Cataloging-in-Publication Data

Nusom, Lynn.
    Christmas in Arizona / by Lynn Nusom.
        p.   cm.
    Includes index.
    1. Christmas cookery.   2. Cookery—Arizona
    3. Christmas-Arizona.   I. Title
TX739.2.C45N86   1992   641.5'68—dc20   92-32251
ISBN 0-914846-65-5   CIP

Printed in the United States of America

Second Printing ©1995

Information in this book is deemed to be authentic and accurate by author and publisher. However, they disclaim any liability incurred in connection with the use of information appearing in this book.

Golden West Publishers, Inc.
4113 N. Longview Ave.
Phoenix, AZ 85014, USA

(602) 265-4392

Golden West Publishers books are available at special discounts to schools, clubs, organizations and businesses for use as fund-raisers, premiums and special promotions. Send inquiry to Director of Marketing.

Christmas in Arizona

Contents

Dedication

This book is dedicated with heartfelt thanks to my wife, Guylyn Morris Nusom, whom I met in Arizona.

Her assistance with all phases of the preparation of this book, including recipe creation, recipe testing, research, proofreading and finding photographic and historic materials was invaluable.

Acknowledgements

My sincere gratitude to Cheryl Thornburg for her editorial efforts and to Anita Worthington and Marjorie Day for their help with the research material.

Christmas in Arizona Celebrations

PHOENIX

Saguaro Festival of Lights - The Foothills, Chandler

International Christmas - Valley Bank Center Concourse, Phoenix

Tempe's Home Town Holiday Festival
Hayden Square Amphitheater, Tempe

An Arizona Christmas - Mesa Community Center Plaza

Noche de las Luminarias - Desert Botanical Garden, Phoenix

Old Town Tempe Fall Festival of the Arts - Old Town Tempe

The Phoenician Resort's Annual Tree Lighting Ceremony
The Phoenician Resort, Scottsdale

Annual Kivel Ball - Arizona Biltmore - Phoenix

Zoobilee - The Phoenix Zoo

Fiesta of Light - Jefferson Street
Central Avenue to Fifth Avenue - Phoenix

Fiesta Bowl Parade - Phoenix

Tour de Noel: A Holiday Home Tour and Tasting
The Phoenician Resort, Scottsdale

Festival of Trees and Marketplace - Phoenix Art Museum

Annual Indian Market - Pueblo Grande Museum - Phoenix

Victorian Holiday Celebration and Craft Fair
Heritage Square, Phoenix

Holiday Light Tours - The Phoenix Parks, Recreation, Phoenix

Rawhide's Family Desert New Year's Eve Celebration
Rawhide, Scottsdale

The Nutcracker - Gammage Auditorium
Tempe & Symphony Hall, Phoenix

Christmas Festival - Carefree/Cavecreek

more: *Christmas in Arizona* Celebrations

Christmas Lights - Arizona Temple Visitors Center, Mesa
Fall Festival of the Arts - Tempe
Tree Lighting and Concert - Scottsdale, Scottsdale Mall
Cowboy Christmas...Poetry, Singin' and Pictures - Wickenburg
Fiesta de Tumacacori
Tumacacori National Monument, Tumacacori, AZ

TUCSON
Fiesta de Guadalupe - Tucson, (DeGrazia Gallery)
Holiday in Lights - Downtown Tucson
Annual Gift Extravaganza - Holiday Inn Broadway
Madrigal Dinner - University of Arizona Student Union Ballroom
Children's Christmas Party - John C. Fremont House Museum
Christmas Everyday
Arizona Children's Theatre Company
Territorial Holidays - John C. Fremont House Museum
Fourth Avenue Street Fair - Fourth Avenue Merchants Association
Winterhaven Festival of the Lights - Ft. Lowell & Country Club
Christmas in the Desert - Park Mall Center
Luminaria Nights - 2150 N. Alvernon Garden

STATEWIDE EVENTS
Christmas Apple Festival - Willcox
Christmas Boat Parade of Lights
Lake Havasu City
Festival of Lights Boat Parade - Wahweap Bay, Lake Powell
Courthouse Lighting and Christmas Parade - Prescott
Territorial Florence Christmas - Clark House - Florence
"Red Rock Fantasy" and the Festival of Lights - Sedona
The Festival of Lights - Tubac
Fiesta Navidad - Tubac

CHAPTER ONE

The Missions of Arizona

The fabled missions of Arizona have played an important role in the development of Christianity and the Christmas celebrations of the Southwest. When the invading Spaniards came into Arizona they discovered Indians dwelling in hogans (dome-shaped mud and grass huts) and rectangular open-sided shelters made of poles and the adobe pueblos that the Hopis lived in.

The priests or padres that came into the region in the last part of the seventeenth century started building missions in the southern part of Arizona and they encouraged the Indians to construct villages around the missions.

The priests imitated the styles and designs of the missions in Mexico. However, they were unable to find artisans that could accurately duplicate these missions and this, coupled with the climate and topographic nature of Arizona, led them to build low shaded cloisters with massive walls and patios.

Most of the mission churches were built in a straight rectangular shape; however, San Xavier del Bac was built in the cruciform manner. Set nine miles south of Tucson, the mission is built of burned brick covered with white lime plaster. The facade is Spanish baroque and the altar is adorned with rich carvings and painted ornaments. Legend has it that this altar also once boasted many silver objects made from silver mined near Tucson.

San Xavier del Bac dubbed "the white dove of the desert" has been a proud memorial to the past and to Father Kino, its founder. It is acclaimed as one of the finest examples of mission architecture in the United States. San Xavier is one of the oldest churches still in use in the United States. The Franciscan brothers give daily lecture tours to visitors (except Sunday). Celebrations and religious festivities are held in October and December. The mission's founding is celebrated every year in April and is a major part of the colorful and exciting Tucson Festival which lasts all month.

Started by Father Kino in 1700, San Xavier was plundered in 1751, and soon after that was destroyed by Apache raids. Though the mission was abandoned for a time, rebuilding started several years later and the mission was finally completed in 1797.

Father Kino was one of the most important personages in Arizona's history. Born to Italian parents in the Tyrolean Alps, he took his training as a Jesuit in Bavaria. The family name was Chini but he Hispanicized it to Kino . His dream was to follow a cousin to the Far East to be a missionary but, instead, he was assigned to the Sonoran desert in 1687.

In the twenty-four years that were to follow he made some forty trips throughout the area, established twenty-four new missions and made the best map of the Southwest available for the next two hundred years. He was a fierce defender, protector and teacher of the Indians of Arizona. He taught them how to be cowboys and raise good strains of cattle, sheep, and horses; he introduced them to new varieties of vegetables and grains, and ministered to their needs both spiritual and physical.

Of the many missions he established, seven of them were in what is now Arizona but only three—San Xavier, Tumacacori, and Guevavi —were still in operation when he died in 1711.

Tumacacori, set against the backdrop of the Santa Rita Mountains, remains a symbol of the courage and faith of the early missionary priests such as Father Kino.

After Father Kino left, the building of Tumacacori was continued by Father Gutierrez who was once buried beneath the sanctuary floor on the left side of the altar. But when the mission was abandoned in 1840, his remains were moved to San Xavier. After a series of Apache raids, Tumacacori was abandoned as an active church in the mid-1800's. Stories of buried treasure and rich hordes of silver buried in Tumacacori attracted treasure hunters who pillaged the mission.

This adobe church is a hundred feet long and over fifty feet wide. The remnants of the Spanish Renaissance style in the architecture can be seen in the stately ruins. In 1908 the mission was made a national monument, and today's visitors can experience what it must have been like during Christmas celebrations two centuries ago when the priests and Indians came together in the house of worship that they had worked so hard to build.

These missions, along with the ruins of San Cayetano de Calabazas and Los Santos Angeles de Guevavi, give us a sense of the indelible imprint the Spanish missionaries made on the territory that is now Arizona.

Appetizers

AVOCADO DIP   4

CHILE NUTS   4

CHILE SALSA   5

GREEN TOMATO AND CHILE RELISH   5

ARTICHOKE DIP   6

CHRISTMAS EVE CHILE SPREAD   6

TUBAC BEAN DIP   7

GREEN CHILE CHUTNEY &
CREAM CHEESE APPETIZER   7

QUESADILLAS   8

TOMBSTONE PEANUTS   9

PICANTE OLIVES   9

CREAMY GUACAMOLE   9

Avocado Dip

When out-of-state friends and relatives come to visit over the Christmas holidays, we often make a point of preparing the following dip before going on those Christmas lights sightseeing trips. Stored in the refrigerator, it is ready for us to dive into the minute we get home.

2 medium size AVOCADOS, peeled and chopped
1 Tbsp. LEMON JUICE
1 (8 oz.) pkg. CREAM CHEESE, at room temperature
1/4 cup ONION, chopped
1/2 tsp. SALT
1 clove GARLIC, minced
1/4 tsp. TABASCO® SAUCE
1/2 cup GREEN CHILE, chopped
1 ripe TOMATO, finely chopped

Blend all the ingredients <u>except</u> the tomato in a food processor until smooth. Stir in the tomato and serve with tortilla chips or fresh vegetables.

Yield: Approx. 2 cups.

Chile Nuts

Nuts have been a traditional part of Christmas in our household as long as I can remember. But it wasn't until we celebrated Christmas in Arizona that we learned how to make them "sit up and sing."

2 cups SALTED PEANUTS
1/4 cup WORCESTERSHIRE SAUCE
1/2 tsp. CAYENNE PEPPER

Spread the peanuts in a baking pan. Sprinkle Worchestershire sauce and cayenne over the nuts and stir until evenly distributed. Bake in a 250 degree oven for 30 minutes or until Worcestershire sauce is absorbed.

Chile Salsa

This recipe uses tomatillos, which are small green Mexican tomatoes that are available in most supermarkets. Serve it with your Christmas turkey, duck or goose for a truly great southwestern taste.

2 lg. RIPE RED TOMATOES, diced
4 TOMATILLOS, diced
1/2 lg. WHITE ONION, finely chopped
1 JALAPEÑO, seeded and chopped
1 clove GARLIC, run through a garlic press
2 Tbsp. OLIVE OIL
1 Tbsp. WINE VINEGAR
1 Tbsp. fresh CILANTRO, chopped
1/2 tsp. SALT
1/2 tsp. ground BLACK PEPPER
1/4 tsp. ground OREGANO

Mix all the ingredients together and chill.

Makes approximately 2 cups.

Green Tomato and Chile Relish

Many Arizona residents have deep southern roots. A green tomato relish has always been a traditional part of the Christmas goodies laid out by our numerous southern relatives. We added the green chile for that Arizona feel.

1 cup GREEN CHILE, chopped
2 large GREEN TOMATOES, peeled and chopped
1 clove GARLIC, minced
1 Tbsp. fresh CILANTRO, chopped
1 Tbsp. LIME or LEMON JUICE

Mix together chile, tomato, garlic and cilantro and finely chop. Stir in the juice, cover, and refrigerate.

Makes approximately 1 cup.

Artichoke Dip

1 clove GARLIC, minced
1/2 tsp. DRY MUSTARD
1/2 tsp. ANCHOVY PASTE
2 Tbsp. DRY VERMOUTH
1 cup SOUR CREAM
1/4 cup MAYONNAISE
6 ARTICHOKE HEARTS, chopped
1/2 tsp. ground WHITE PEPPER
1 Tbsp. PARSLEY, chopped
2 Tbsp. GREEN ONIONS, chopped
2 Tbsp. PIMENTOS, chopped

Blend the garlic, mustard, anchovy paste, vermouth, sour cream, mayonnaise and artichoke hearts. Stir in pepper, parsley, green onions, and pimentos. Refrigerate for 2 hours before serving. Excellent with tortilla chips.

Makes approximately 2 cups.

Christmas Eve Chile Spread

Nothing is quite so special to many Arizona families as La Noche Buena - Christmas Eve, when they open wide the doors of their homes to friends and neighbors and serve all sorts of goodies. This spread will help set a festive table.

1/2 cup MAYONNAISE
1 package (8 oz) CREAM CHEESE
1/3 cup PECANS, chopped
2 Tbsp. GREEN CHILE, chopped
1 Tbsp. PARSLEY, chopped
1/4 cup ONION, finely chopped
1 tsp. SAFFLOWER

Mix all ingredients together and serve with party rye, pumpernickel or crackers.

Tubac Bean Dip

1 can (15 ounce) REFRIED BEANS
1/2 cup SALSA (your favorite brand)
1/4 cup dry WHITE WINE (add more to thin,
     if necessary)
2 Tbsp. fresh CILANTRO, chopped
MONTEREY JACK CHEESE grated

Stir the beans, salsa, wine and cilantro together in a frying pan until heated through. Sprinkle with the cheese and serve warm.

Green Chile Chutney
and
Cream Cheese Appetizer

A great chum of ours who was born in India now lives in Phoenix and insists that we make chutney for him during the holidays. I decided that the recipe had to have chile and tequila in it to give it that Arizona flavor.

4 oz. GREEN CHILE chopped
2 JALAPENOS, stems removed, finely chopped (or more to taste)
1 cup TOMATOES, peeled and cooked, with the juice
2 Tbsp. WHITE ONION, finely chopped
1 clove GARLIC, finely chopped
JUICE OF ONE LIME
1 oz. TEQUILA
1/2 tsp. SALT
1/2 tsp. ground CUMIN
1/4 tsp. ground CLOVES
8 oz. package CREAM CHEESE

Mix all ingredients together, <u>except</u> the cream cheese, in a saucepan and cook over low heat for 30 minutes. Let cool, then refrigerate for at least 4 hours. Place the cream cheese on a serving plate, pour the chutney over the cream cheese and spread on crackers.

Serves: Approximately 24.

Quesadillas

Just like songs which are "golden oldies" food often evokes remembrances of places and people. Whenever we make this simple appetizer it invariably brings back memories of a Christmas Eve once spent at Mt. Lemon in a log cabin in front of a roaring fire.

1/2 lb. grated MONTEREY JACK CHEESE
4 oz. GREEN CHILE, chopped
2 Tbsp. SOUR CREAM
1/2 tsp. GARLIC SALT
1/2 tsp. CUMIN
Several dashes of TABASCO® SAUCE
24 small, cocktail-sized TORTILLAS
sliced JALAPEÑOS (to taste)

Mix the cheese, chile, sour cream, garlic salt, cumin and Tabasco together. Spoon a small amount of the mixture on the tortillas. Sprinkle with sliced jalapeños, if desired. Fold the tortillas over and pinch the ends so the cheese and sour cream mixture won't leak out. Put on a lightly greased baking or cookie sheet and bake for 15 - 20 minutes at 350 degrees or until nicely browned. Serve warm.

Serves: approximately 24.

Tombstone Peanuts

1 Tbsp. PEANUT OIL
1 jar (12 oz.) or 2 1/2 cups DRY ROASTED PEANUTS
1/2 tsp. GARLIC POWDER
1/2 tsp. ground GINGER
1/2 tsp. CAYENNE PEPPER

Heat the oil in a large frying pan, add the rest of the ingredients and cook over medium high heat, stirring for 3 - 4 minutes. Remove from heat, let cool and serve.

Yield: 2 1/2 cups.

Picante Olives

1 can (7 oz.) LARGE PITTED RIPE OLIVES, drained
2 CLOVES GARLIC, minced
2 HOT CHILE PEPPERS (Pepin or Serano), seeded, chopped
2 Tbsp. OLIVE OIL

Drain olives and put with the garlic cloves, peppers and olive oil in a covered dish and store in the refrigerator for 2 - 3 days.

Creamy Guacamole

Just as cranberry sauce is an essential part of a Yankee Christmas dinner, many Arizonans don't feel that the holiday meal is complete without guacamole.

1/2 cup SOUR CREAM
1 Tbsp. WHITE WINE
2 lg. AVOCADOS, peeled and mashed
1/2 tsp. GARLIC POWDER
1/2 tsp. SALT
1/2 tsp. ground WHITE PEPPER
JUICE OF ONE LIME
dash of TABASCO®

Mix all the ingredients together and serve with tortilla chips.

Tucson, Arizona

Arizona Daily Star

December 22, 1912

The Night Before Christmas

by Wilbur D. Nesbit

" 'Tis the night before Christmas"
  I whisper the rhyme
And wander in fancy
  To "once on a time."
I see the big fireplace,
  The girls and the boys,
The long, heaped-up stockings,
  The drums and the toys.
" 'Tis the night before Christmas"
  So old, and so new!
With all of its dreamings
  So good and so true.
I see all the faces
  Forgotten so long
And out of the twilight
  There murmurs a song.
" 'Tis the night before Christmas"
  And here, by my grate,
The past rises, glowing,
  The years lose their weight,
The boy-days come trooping
  At memory's call,
And gleam in the embers
  That flicker and fall.

" 'Tis the night before Christmas"
  Ah, could I but clutch
The gold of my fancies!
  T'would go at my touch!
The shouts and the laughter
  Now sweet to my ear
Would shrink to a silence
  Too deep and too drear.
" 'Tis the night before Christmas"
  Remembrances stir
As sweet as the cherished
  Frankincense and myrrh.
And hark!   As the visions
  Grow dim to the sight.
There comes, "Merry Christmas!
  And boy-days, good night!"

Beverages

HOT BUTTERED RUM   12

FLAGSTAFF FOG   12

TANGELO SUNRISE   12

ARIZONA EYE OPENER   13

MANGO MADNESS   13

PATAGONIA TEQUILA   13

KAHLUA SMOOTHIE   14

MY MARGARITA   14

CHAMPAGNE PUNCH   14

Hot Buttered Rum

What could be more perfect after a snowy day on the trails than this warming drink?

1 qt. VANILLA ICE CREAM
1/2 lb. BUTTER or MARGARINE, at room temperature
1 lb. BROWN SUGAR
1 Tbsp. ground NUTMEG

Mix the ice cream, butter, sugar and nutmeg together. Store in freezer until ready to use.

1 Tbsp. of the ICE CREAM MIXTURE
2 oz. RUM
HOT WATER
NUTMEG

Put a tablespoon of the ice cream mixture in a mug. Stir in the rum, add hot water to the top of the mug and stir. Sprinkle with nutmeg, if desired.

Flagstaff Fog

1 qt. FRENCH VANILLA ICE CREAM
1 cup BOURBON
1 cup COLD COFFEE

Put the ingredients into a blender and blend well. Pour into individual stemmed glasses and serve garnished with chocolate curls.

Serves 4.

Tangelo Sunrise

Juice of 3 TANGELOS
1 oz. TEQUILA
1/2 tsp. LIME JUICE

1/2 tsp. GRENADINE
CRUSHED ICE
LIME SLICE

Put all the ingredients, except lime slice, in a blender and blend until smooth. Pour into a large cocktail glass and serve with a slice of lime.

Serves 1.

Arizona Eye Opener

This is the southwestern version of the Bloody Mary.

1 oz. TEQUILA
TOMATO JUICE
Juice of 1/2 LIME
Dash of TABASCO®

Dash of CELERY SALT
Dash of ground BLACK PEPPER
LIME SLICE

Pour the tequila over ice cubes in a tall glass. Pour in tomato juice almost to the top of the glass, add the lime juice, Tabasco, celery salt and black pepper and stir. Garnish with a lime slice and serve.

Mango Madness

One December all the travel posters shouted, "Spend the Christmas Holidays in the Caribbean!." We saved the airfare and savored this aptly named libation right here in Arizona.

1/4 MANGO (approx. 4 oz.), peeled or cut into chunks
1 1/2 oz. RUM
1 oz. ORANGE FLAVORED LIQUEUR
1/2 cup PINEAPPLE JUICE
CRUSHED ICE
MANGO CHUNKS
PINEAPPLE CHUNKS
MARASCHINO CHERRIES

Put all the ingredients in a blender and blend until smooth. Pour into a large glass and garnish with a mini-kabob made of chucks of mango, pineapple and maraschino cherries.

Serves 1.

Patagonia Tequila

Makes a great "hot" Christmas Gift

1 Bottle WHITE TEQUILA
2 JALAPENOS, seeded, cut in strips

Poke the jalapeno strips into the bottle of tequila. Cap, and store for a least a week. Serve straight with lemon and salt or use to make Bloody Marys.

Kahlúa® Smoothie

2 scoops COFFEE ICE CREAM	1/2 cup MILK
2 oz. KAHLÚA®	CRUSHED ICE
1 oz. BRANDY	Dash Ground NUTMEG

Put all the ingredients into a blender and blend until smooth. Pour into glasses and top with a dash of nutmeg.

Serves 2.

My Margarita

The secret to great margaritas is to keep it simple!

2 oz. WHITE TEQUILA	CRUSHED ICE
1 oz. TRIPLE SEC	COARSE (KOSHER) SALT
1/2 oz. LIME JUICE	SLICE OF LIME

Put all the ingredients, <u>except</u> the salt and lime slice, into a blender and blend until smooth. Put a little Triple Sec on your finger and run it around the rim of a cocktail glass. Pour some coarse salt into a saucer, and place the rim of the cocktail glass in the salt. Fill the glass with the margarita and serve garnished with a slice of lime.

Serves 1.

Champagne Punch

Perfect party punch for the holidays!

Sliced MANGOES
Sliced STRAWBERRIES
1 can (12 oz.) FROZEN ORANGE CONCENTRATE
1 cup ORANGE FLAVORED LIQUEUR
3 bottles (750 ml. each) DRY or BRUT CHAMPAGNE (chilled)
2 bottles (28 oz. each) CLUB SODA (chilled)

Put the fruit in the bottom of a ring mold, fill with water and freeze. Unmold and place in the bottom of a punch bowl. Pour in the orange juice, orange flavored liqueur, then the champagne and, finally, the club soda.

CHAPTER TWO

Las Posadas & Piñatas

The reenactment of Mary and Joseph's search for a place to stay in Bethlehem on the night of Christ's birth has long been an historic and integral part of the Christmas celebration in Arizona.

Originally the tradition began on December 15th or 16th and lasted until Christmas Eve. Accompanied by a group of children carrying candles or torches and singing carols and hymns, two people representing Mary and Joseph went from house to house seeking admission. Carved figures of the holy couple in search of an inn were carried through the streets. Each night, the weary travelers were finally given shelter and refreshments.

Today, the celebration of the Posada most often happens on December 23rd or on Christmas Eve when a group of people go from door-to-door, often singing Christmas carols perhaps with a guitar or two for accompaniment. At many of the homes the revelers are invited in and served libations and all sorts of good food.

The children look forward with anticipation to the posada because they know that at the last home they visit the custom of breaking the piñata will take place.

The little ones gather around a filled piñata that is suspended so it will swing over their heads. The children take turns at being blindfolded and swinging a stick in an attempt to break it open until one lucky youngster connects with the piñata hard enough to split it open.

Then there is a scramble for the hard candies and gifts that spill out onto the floor and everyone shares in the loot.

In the past, piñatas were clay bowls or "ollas" that broke easily when hit. Now, piñatas are constructed of papier-mache, covered with brightly-colored, shredded tissue paper and come in a huge variety of figures such as donkeys, stars, Santa Claus, unicorns, chile peppers, and even cartoon characters.

The lyrics of "Las Posadas" tells the simple story of the holy couple in search of lodging in Bethlehem on the night Christ was born. Shown below is the melody followed by an English translation of the song.

LAS POSADAS

¿ Quién les da - po - sa - da a es - tos pe - re - gri - nos, que vie - nen can - sa - dos de - an - dar los ca - mi - nos? Por más que di - gá - is que ve - nís ren - di - dos, no da - mos po - sa - da a des - co - no - ci - dos.

(Reprinted from "*El Mundo Español*" Vol. II, 1942, by permission of D. C. Heath and Company)

Las Posadas

(English translation)

Saint Joseph: Who will give lodging to these pilgrims, who are tired out from traveling the highways?

Innkeeper: However much you may say that you are worn out, we do not give lodging to strangers.

Saint Joseph: In the name of heaven, I beg of you lodging, since my beloved wife can travel no longer.

Innkeeper: There is no lodging here; keep on moving. I cannot open to you, don't be stupid.

Saint Joseph: Don't be inhuman and have pity, for the God of the Heavens will reward you for it.

Innkeeper: Now you may go away and not bother me, because if I get mad I'm going to beat you.

Saint Joseph: We come worn out from Nazareth; I am a carpenter by the name of Joseph.

Innkeeper: Your name doesn't concern me; let me sleep, since I have already told you that we are not to open to you.

Saint Joseph: Lodging, dear Innkeeper, for only one night, the Queen of the Heavens begs of you.

Innkeeper: Well then if she is a queen who asks it, how is it that at night she goes so unattended?

Saint Joseph: My wife is Mary, the Queen of the Heavens; mother she will be of the Divine Word.

Innkeeper: Is it you, Joseph and your wife Mary? Enter pilgrims; I did not know you.

Saint Joseph: Happy be this house that gives us lodging; may God always give you your sacred happiness.

Innkeeper: Lodging we give you with much happiness; enter, honest Joseph, enter with Mary.

Chorus: (from without), Enter saintly pilgrims; receive this ovation, not from this poor dwelling but from my heart.

Chorus: (from within), This night is (made) of happiness, of pleasure, and of rejoicing, because we give lodging here to the Mother of the Son of God.

Tucson, Arizona **Arizona Daily Star** December 22, 1912

The Stag Grill

Zeigel & Andlauer, Proprietors

CHRISTMAS MENU

THE BEST FOOD IS CULINARY ART

Oysters on Half Shell Oysters any style

Steamed Little Neck Clams

RELISHES

Salted Almonds Stuffed Celery Leaves

Tomatoes a la Russe Sardines l'Hulle

Canape en Bellevue Bismark Dill Pickles

Queen Olives are Ripe Sardelles a'la Diables

SOUP

Consomme Double Cream Florentine

FISH

Baby Brook Trout, sauce Hollandaise

Catalina Salad Dabs a la Colbert

Stuffed Smelts, Bordelaise

Lobster a la Americaine, or Cold or Broiled

ENTREES

Home Made Goose Liver a la Strasburgoise

Sweet Bread a la Richelleu

Fillet Mignon, a la Perigue

Fried Eastern Frog Legs, Brown Butter

Belgian Hare Saute au Champigon

ROASTS

Suckling Pig, Oyster Dressing

Corn Fed Young Turkey, Cranberry Sauce

VEGETABLES

Petit Pois au Beure Pommes Noisette

DESSERT

Christmas Plum Pudding Savarin au Rhum

Pie a la Mode Mince Pie

American Cheese Rockfort Cheese

Camembert and Swiss Cheese

Special Christmas Wine and Demi Tasse

22 North Church Street Phone Red 1841

Salads

MOLDED AVOCADO SALAD   20
Cream Topping

CHRISTMAS MELON SALAD   21

ARTICHOKE JICAMA SALAD   21
Orange Dressing

CHICKEN ARTICHOKE SALAD   22
Sesame Dressing

SEDONA CHRISTMAS SALAD   23

SALAD OF THE ANGELS   23

CRANBERRY SALAD   24

TOPOPO SALAD   25

Molded Avocado Salad

Many of us often feel like "setting the world on fire" at Christmas time. If you want to join in, just add the optional jalapeno to the topping for this recipe.

1 pkg. (6 oz.) LIME JELLO®
1/2 tsp. SALT
2 cups BOILING WATER
1 1/2 cups COLD WATER
2 Tbsp. LEMON JUICE
2 AVOCADOS, peeled and mashed
3/4 cup MAYONNAISE

Dissolve Jello and salt in boiling water. Stir in the cold water and chill in the refrigerator until slightly thickened. Stir lemon juice into mashed avocados. Add avocado mixture and mayonnaise to gelatin until well blended. Spoon into a ring mold and refrigerate until set. To serve, unmold onto a serving plate, pour the following topping into a small bowl and place in the center of the avocado mold.

Topping

1 pkg. (8 oz.) CREAM CHEESE
1 cup SOUR CREAM
1 Tbsp. LIME JUICE
1/4 tsp. CAYENNE PEPPER
CILANTRO
SLICED JALAPENOS (optional)

Blend all ingredients together, <u>except</u> cilantro, in a food processor or mixer until smooth and creamy (adding more sour cream, if necessary). Spoon into a small bowl that will fit into the center of the avocado mold. Garnish with sprig of cilantro.

Serves 6 - 8.

Christmas Melon Salad

Although buying various melons for Christmas time was not possible a few years ago, they are now available in many places. This makes a delightful salad for a Christmas buffet or it can be served as a dessert.

1 **cup SUGAR**
2 **cups WATER**
2 **Tbsp. LEMON JUICE**
2 **Tbsp. PRESERVED GINGER, finely chopped**
2 **cups WATERMELON BALLS**
2 **cups HONEYDEW BALLS**

Stir the sugar and water together in a saucepan and bring to a boil, reduce heat and cook for 5 - 6 minutes. Add the lemon juice and ginger. Let cool to room temperature. Pour over melon balls and chill in the refrigerator for an hour before serving.

Serves 4 - 6.

Artichoke Jicama Salad

1 **cup ARTICHOKE HEARTS, drained and halved**
1 **cup MANDARIN ORANGES, drained**
1 **medium size JICAMA, peeled and thinly sliced**
1 **bunch LEAF LETTUCE, washed, dried and torn**
      into bite-size pieces

Combine in a salad bowl and toss with the following dressing.

Orange Dressing

1/2 cup fresh ORANGE JUICE
1/4 cup fresh LIME JUICE
1 1/2 tablespoons OLIVE OIL
1/2 teaspoon SALT
1/2 teaspoon ground BLACK PEPPER
1 teaspoon grated ORANGE PEEL

Mix all the ingredients and toss with the Artichoke and Jicama Salad.

Serves 4 - 6.

Chicken Artichoke Salad

1 large head of LEAF LETTUCE
2 cups WHITE CHICKEN MEAT, cooked and diced
1 cup ARTICHOKE HEARTS, drained & coarsely chopped
1 cup CELERY, finely diced
1/2 cup RED ONION, finely sliced

Wash, pat or drain dry, and tear the lettuce into bite-size pieces. Combine with rest of the ingredients in a salad bowl. Toss lightly with the following dressing:

Sesame Dressing

1/2 tsp. LEMON PEEL grated
1/2 tsp. PREPARED MUSTARD
1/2 cup DRY WHITE WINE
1 Tbsp. SOY SAUCE
1 Tbsp. TOASTED SESAME OIL
1 Tbsp. SUGAR

Mix all the ingredients together well, pour over the salad and toss lightly.

Serves 4.

The following appeared on the front page of the Christmas Eve Edition

Tucson, Arizona	*Arizona Daily Star*	December 23, 1890

With Greetings of the J.P.L. Popular Store.

Christmas in All Lands

He reigns the round world o'er
This good and jolly king,
'neath austral sun's downpour
they give him welcoming

And in the frozen North
the seeker of the whale
brims cup and sendeth forth
to Santa Claus a hail.

The dusky cotter, too,
the man who plenty has -
all share the common view,
"Gold bless St. Nicholas."

And here in Arizona, far as in this
Southland clime,
A merry Christmas to our friends
as well as all mankind,
For it was out of skies like those
which arch our mounts and plains.
The chorus: "Peace on earth, good-
will to man," swept out in
joyous strains
For more than eighteen hundred years
Christmas day has come and gone,
And ten thousand tongues ten thou-
sand times will 'gain repeat the song.

Sedona Christmas Salad

This old-fashioned salad somehow seems right at home in the "new age" world of today's Sedona..

1 cup **RED APPLES, unpeeled and diced**
1 cup **GREEN APPLES, unpeeled and diced**
1 cup **PINEAPPLE CHUNKS**
1/2 cup **CELERY, diced**
1/2 cup **CARROTS, grated**
1 cup **GOLDEN RAISINS**
1 cup **MAYONNAISE**
1/2 cup **DRY WHITE WINE**
1 tsp. dried **MINT LEAVES, crushed**
1 cup **PECANS, chopped**
1 cup **SHARP CHEDDAR CHEESE, grated**

Place the fruits, vegetables and raisins in a salad bowl. Mix together the mayonnaise, wine, and mint leaves. Pour over the vegetables and toss lightly. Add the pecans and cheese, lightly toss again and serve.

Serves 6 - 8.

Salad of the Angels

1 can (20 oz.) **PINEAPPLE CHUNKS, drained**
1 can (11 oz.) **MANDARIN ORANGES**
1 cup **COCONUT**
1 cup **SOUR CREAM**
1 cup small **MARSHMALLOWS**
1 cup **SEEDLESS GRAPES, cut in half**
1/2 tsp. ground **CARDAMON**

Mix all the ingredients together and chill in the refrigerator until ready to serve.

Serves 4 - 6.

Cranberry Salad

1 cup BOILING WATER
3/4 cup ORANGE JUICE
1 (3 oz.) pkg. RED RASPBERRY GELATIN
1 (8 oz.) WHOLE CRANBERRY SAUCE
1 cup APPLES, peeled and diced
1/2 cup CELERY, diced
1/2 cup PECANS, chopped
1/2 cup SOUR CREAM
1 Tbsp. CREME DE MENTHE

Dissolve the gelatin in the boiling water, stir in the orange juice and cranberry sauce. Chill in the refrigerator until the gelatin starts to thicken. Stir in the apples, celery and pecans and spoon into a 4 cup mold. Chill until set. Unmold onto a plate. Garnish with sour cream mixed with creme de menthe.

Serves 4 - 6.

Topopo Salad

This salad, a favorite of mine, is great during the holidays, or any time of the year!

1/2 cup TACO SAUCE or SALSA
2 cups REFRIED BEANS
4 CORN TORTILLAS, fried until crisp or purchased
    as tostada or tapatia shells
8 cups LETTUCE, finely shredded
4 slices SMOKED TURKEY or CHICKEN, cut into strips
4 slices CHEDDAR CHEESE, cut into strips
2 AVOCADOS, peeled, seeded and cut into strips
12 BLACK OLIVES
ITALIAN DRESSING

Mix the salsa with the refried beans and spread 1/4 of the mixture on each tostada shell and place on individual plates. Mound two cups of lettuce (volcano shape) on each shell. Lay turkey strips, cheese strips and avocado strips upright against the lettuce. Top with 3 olives each, pour Italian dressing generously over the salad and serve.

Serves 4.

Soups

CHILLED AVOCADO SOUP   26

CLAM AND CHILE CHOWDER   26

TORTILLA SOUP   27

CHICKEN POSOLE   28

CASA GRANDE GAZPACHO   29

BLACK BEAN SOUP   29

ALBONDIGAS SOUP   30

SHRIMP ALBONDIGAS SOUP   31

SPLIT PEA SOUP   31

MENUDO   32

Chili

CHICKEN NAVY BEAN CHILI   33

CHANDLER CHILI   34

INDIAN CHILI   35

Chilled Avocado Soup

1 medium size ONION,
coarsely chopped
2 large AVOCADOS, peeled
2 Tbsp. LIME JUICE
2 cups MILK

2 cans (14 1/2 oz.) CHICKEN
STOCK
2 cups HALF AND HALF
1/2 tsp. SALT
1/4 tsp. CAYENNE PEPPER

Blend the onions, avocados, lime juice and milk in a blender until smooth. Pour into a saucepan, add the rest of the ingredients and cook over medium heat for 15 to 20 minutes. Remove from the heat and chill in the refrigerator for 6 hours. Serve with sprigs of fresh cilantro.

Serves 4 - 6.

Clam & Chile Chowder

3 Tbsp. BUTTER or MARGARINE
3 Tbsp. FLOUR
2 cups CHICKEN BROTH
2 cups MILK
1 medium size ONION, chopped
3 cans (8 oz. each) MINCED CLAMS with the juice
3 large POTATOES, peeled, cooked and diced
1/2 tsp. SALT
1/2 tsp. ground WHITE PEPPER
1/2 tsp. ground CUMIN
1 tsp. CILANTRO, chopped
1/2 cup GREEN CHILE, chopped
2 cups HALF AND HALF
dash of TABASCO®
chopped CHIVES

Melt the butter in a soup pot. Stir in the flour to make a roux, add the chicken broth and stir over high heat, until smooth. Lower heat and add the onion, clams, potatoes, salt, pepper, cumin, cilantro and green chile. Cook for 30 minutes. Stir in the half and half and Tabasco and cook until the soup is warmed through. Serve the soup garnished with a sprinkling of chopped chives.

Serves 4 - 6.

Tortilla Soup

I like making a pot of this and keeping it on the back burner for drop-in company around the holidays.

2 Tbsp. OLIVE OIL
2 cloves GARLIC, minced
1 medium size ONION, chopped
1 can (#303 - 28 oz.) PEELED TOMATOES, chopped with the juice
1 Tbsp. PARSLEY, chopped
1/2 cup GREEN CHILE, Chopped
1 JALAPENO, seeded and chopped
1 lb. CHICKEN MEAT, cooked, boned and cut into bite-size pieces
6 cups CHICKEN BROTH
Juice of 2 LIMES
1 tsp. fresh CILANTRO, chopped
1/2 tsp. ground BLACK PEPPER
1 tsp. SALT
TORTILLA CHIPS
LIME SLICES

Sauté the garlic and onion in the oil in a soup pot until the onion is tender, add the tomatoes, green chile, parsley, jalapeno, and chicken and cook for 5 minutes. Add the chicken broth, lime juice, cilantro, pepper, and salt and cook for 30 minutes.

Break the tostada shells into pieces and divide in the bottoms of soup bowls. Pour the soup on top of the tortilla chips, garnish with lime slices and serve.

Serves 6 - 8.

Chicken Posole

This popular dish combines both Mexican and Indian cultures and is a "must" on the Christmas menu of a great many Arizona households.

Although traditionally made with pork, lamb or beef the use of chicken or turkey is becoming more common in this wonderful dish.

2 lbs. CHICKEN or TURKEY MEAT, cooked and ground
   or cooked and cut into bite-size pieces
2 cans (#303 WHITE HOMINY or 1 # 10), drained
6 cups CHICKEN BROTH
1 medium size ONION, chopped
1/2 cup GREEN CHILE, chopped
   (or use jalapeños for a "hotter" taste)
2 cloves GARLIC, minced
1 tsp. ground OREGANO
1 tsp. ground BLACK PEPPER
1 Tbsp. RED CHILE POWDER
1 tsp. ground CUMIN
juice of one LIME

Put all the ingredients into a large pot and cook for 1 hour over low heat until all the flavors are blended. Serve with red chile sauce and tostadas.

Serves 4 - 6.

Casa Grande Gazpacho

6 lg. ripe TOMATOES, peeled and chopped
2 medium size CUCUMBERS, peeled and chopped
1 GREEN BELL PEPPER, seeded and chopped
2 ribs CELERY, chopped
4 GREEN ONIONS, chopped
2 cups TOMATO or V-8 JUICE
1 JALAPEÑO, seeded and chopped (optional)
1/4 cup WHITE WINE
1 clove GARLIC, minced
1/2 tsp. SALT
1/2 tsp. ground BLACK PEPPER
JUICE of one LIME
LIME WEDGES or SLICES

Mix all the ingredients, except the lime wedges, together and chill in the refrigerator for at least 2 hours before serving. Serve garnished with lime wedges or slices.

Serves 4 - 6.

Black Bean Soup

2 Tbsp. OLIVE OIL
2 Tbsp. BUTTER or MARGARINE
3 GREEN ONIONS, chopped
1 ONION, chopped
2 cloves GARLIC, minced
1 Tbsp. PARSLEY, chopped
4 cups BLACK BEANS, cooked and drained
6 cups CHICKEN STOCK
1/4 cup WHITE WINE or DRY VERMOUTH
1 tsp. ground BLACK PEPPER
1 tsp. SALT
TABASCO® to taste
LIME SLICES
JALAPEÑO SLICES

Saute the green onion, onion and garlic in the oil and butter until the onion is soft. Add the rest of the ingredients and cook over medium heat for 30 - 45 minutes. Serve garnished with lime slices and sliced jalapenos.

Serves 6 - 8.

Albondigas Soup

This traditional Mexican soup is often served as part of the celebration of the Feast of Guadalupe.

2 Tbsp. OLIVE OIL
2 Tbsp. BUTTER or MARGARINE
1 clove GARLIC, minced
1 ONION, chopped
1 Tbsp. FRESH PARSLEY, chopped
1 lb. GROUND BEEF
1/2 lb. GROUND PORK
1 cup DRY BREAD CRUMBS
1/2 tsp. ground CUMIN
1 tsp. ground RED CHILE POWDER
1/2 tsp. SALT
1/2 tsp. ground BLACK PEPPER
2 EGGS, lightly beaten
2 cans (10 1/2 oz. each) BEEF BROTH
4 cups WATER
2 Tbsp. TOMATO SAUCE
1/4 cup RED WINE
2 BAY LEAVES, broken in half
LIME WEDGES

Saute the garlic, onion and parsley in the oil and butter until the onion is soft. Remove from the frying pan and reserve the oil. Mix the onion with the ground beef, ground pork, bread crumbs, cumin, chile powder, salt, pepper and eggs and form into small balls. Fry the meatballs in the reserved oil (adding more, if necessary) until they are browned on all sides.

Pour the beef broth and water into a large soup pot, add the tomato sauce, wine and bay leaves and bring to a boil. Reduce the heat, add the meat balls and cook over medium high heat for 20 minutes. Remove bay leaves and serve garnished with lime wedges.

Serves 6 - 8.

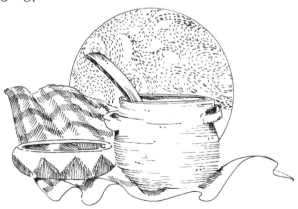

Shrimp Albondigas Soup

3 GREEN ONIONS, chopped
1 clove GARLIC, minced
1 rib CELERY, chopped
1 Tbsp. FRESH PARSLEY, chopped
3 Tbsp. OLIVE OIL
2 cans (4 1/2 oz.) SMALL SHRIMP, drained
1/2 cup SEASONED DRY BREAD CRUMBS
1 EGG
2 cans (14 1/2 oz. each) CHICKEN BROTH
1 Tbsp. LEMON JUICE
1 tsp. DILL WEED, chopped
1/2 tsp. ground WHITE PEPPER

Saute the onions, garlic, celery and parsley in the oil, then mix with the shrimp, bread crumbs and egg and form into small balls. Fry the shrimp balls in the leftover oil (adding more if necessary) until lightly browned on all sides.

Pour the broth into a soup pot, add the lemon juice, dill weed, and pepper and bring to a boil. Turn down the heat, add the shrimp balls and cook until the balls are warmed through.

Serves 4.

Split Pea Soup

2 cups SPLIT PEAS
4 cups COLD WATER
2 cups CHICKEN BROTH
1 ONION, chopped
1 CARROT, chopped
1 Tbsp. FRESH PARSLEY, chopped
2 ribs CELERY with the LEAVES, chopped
1 clove GARLIC, chopped
1 tsp. ground BLACK PEPPER
1/2 tsp. SALT

Soak the peas in the cold water overnight. Drain, and put the peas into a soup pot with 6 cups of new water and the chicken broth. Stir in the onion, carrot, parsley, celery and garlic and cook over low heat for 2 hours, stirring occasionally. Stir in salt and pepper. Wonderful served with corn bread.

Serves 6 - 8.

Menudo

Many Arizonans swear by this as a great remedy for a holiday hangover.

2 **Tbsp. OLIVE OIL**
2 **YELLOW ONIONS, chopped**
3 **cloves GARLIC, run through a garlic press**
1 **cup RED CHILE POWDER**
1 **tsp. OREGANO**
1 **tsp. ground BLACK PEPPER**
1 **tsp. ground CUMIN**
1 **tsp. SALT**
4 **qts. WATER**
1 **can (#10) HOMINY**
2 **lbs. TRIPE, well washed and cut into 1" pieces**
1/4 **cup fresh CILANTRO, chopped**
4 **GREEN ONIONS, finely chopped**
LIME WEDGES

Saute onions in olive oil until soft. Add garlic and spices and stir. Pour water into a large soup kettle, add the hominy, tripe and the onions with the spices. Add the cilantro and simmer, over medium heat, for 4 hours or until the tripe is tender.

Serve in soup bowls with green onions sprinkled on top and lime wedges served on the side.

Serves 10 - 12.

Chicken, Navy Bean Chili

This is my version of white chili.

2 Tbsp. BUTTER or MARGARINE
2 Tbsp. OLIVE OIL
1 medium size ONION, chopped
1 clove GARLIC, minced
2 tsp. RED CHILE POWDER
1 tsp. BASIL
1/2 tsp. ground OREGANO
1 tsp. CILANTRO, chopped
4 CHICKEN BREASTS, boned, skinned and cut into cubes
3 cups CHICKEN BROTH
1/4 cup WHITE WINE
2 cans (16 oz.) NAVY BEANS (or other white beans
    such as Great Northern), drained
1 can (28 oz.) CRUSHED TOMATOES
1/2 tsp. SALT
1/2 tsp. ground BLACK PEPPER
TORTILLAS

Melt the butter in a large heavy pot add the oil and let heat for a couple of minutes, then stir in the onion and garlic and cook until the onion is soft. Next, stir in the red chile powder, basil, oregano, and cilantro. Add the cubed chicken and cook until lightly browned. Add the chicken broth, wine, beans, tomatoes, salt and pepper, and cook for 1 hour, stirring occasionally. Serve with warm flour tortillas.

Serves 4 - 6.

Chandler Chili

Chili is the most popular stew served in the United States. This Arizona version has a true Southwestern flavor. See below for other variations

3 Tbsp. OLIVE OIL
1 lg. ONION, chopped
2 cloves GARLIC, minced
1 lb. GROUND ROUND
1/2 tsp. ground OREGANO
1/2 tsp. ground CUMIN
2 Tbsp. RED CHILE POWDER
2 cups CRUSHED TOMATOES
1 Tbsp. PARSLEY, chopped
1 cup WATER

Saute the onion and garlic in the olive oil in a heavy pot or Dutch oven until the onion is soft. Stir in the ground meat and brown it. Then add the oregano, cumin, chile powder, crushed tomatoes, parsley and water and cook for 2 hours over low heat. Add more water, if necessary.

Serves 4 - 6.

VARIATIONS:

Use cubed beef instead of ground beef
Add 1/2 tsp. Nutmeg
Add 1/4 cup of Red Wine
Add jalapeños or jalapeño juice
Add drained, cooked Pinto Beans
Add 1 wedge of Mexican Ibarra® Chocolate

Indian Chili

2 Tbsp. OLIVE OIL
2 Tbsp. BUTTER
1 medium size ONION, chopped
1 clove GARLIC, minced
1 lb. GROUND ROUND
1/2 lb. GROUND PORK
1 Tbsp. RED CHILE POWDER
1 Tbsp. PARSLEY, chopped
1/2 tsp. SALT
1/2 tsp. ground BLACK PEPPER
2 cups CHICKEN BROTH
1 can (30 oz.) HOMINY, drained
2 cups MONTEREY JACK CHEESE, grated

Saute the onion and garlic in the oil and butter until soft. Stir in the beef, pork, chile powder, parsley, salt and pepper until the meat is browned. Stir in the chicken broth and hominy, then layer in a Dutch oven, alternating with the cheese. Bake for 45 minutes in 350 degree oven.

Serves 4 - 6.

This advertisement from the Arizona Daily Star - December 23, 1914 gives us some idea of what was served in Arizona's restaurants some eighty years ago. Note the "affordable" prices.

Rossi's

CHRISTMAS DINNER

Music by Phillips Orchestra
A la Carte
Oysters on Half Shell, 40c

SOUPS
Tortellini de Bologna, 15c   Consomme Clear, 10c

FISH
Fillets of Sea Bass a la Normandia - Hollandaise Sauce, 40c
Parisian Potatoes, 40c

ENTREES
One Oyster Patty, 30c, two 50c
Veal Cutlets Villa Reals, Rossi's Special, 50c
Beef Tornada - Mushroom Maderia, 40c
Milk Fed Chicken, Fried Maryland, 60c

ROASTS
Roast Young Turkey, Chestnut Dressing, Cranberry Sauce, 60c
Roast Young Tame Duck, Apple sauce, 60c
Prime Ribs of Beef au Jus, 40c
Virginia Hams, Champagne Sauce, 40c

COLD MEATS
Pate de Foie Gras, A Spice Jelly, 60c
Boned Turkey - Jelatine

VEGETABLES
Fresh Spinach 15c, Egg Plant, Fried, 15c, Cauliflower in Cream, 15c
Mashed Potatoes
Fresh Artichoke, Mayonnaise Dressing, 30c

SALAD
Fresh Lobster or Crab, 50c   Combination, 25c

DESSERTS
English Plum Pudding - Brandy Sauce, 25c
Metropolitan Ice Cream and Cake, 25c
Fruit Cake 10c   French Pastry 10c   Cream Pie 15c   Coffee 10c

All kinds of Fish, fresh Crab, Lobster and Terrapin.
We can serve you today anything that is served anywhere

CHAPTER THREE

Celebration in the Cities of Arizona

The first Christmas I celebrated in Arizona was as the guest of friends in Tucson. They lived near the university in an elegant older home that boasted two dining rooms. Unfortunately, neither of them either liked to cook or possessed much knowledge of the workings of a kitchen.

Therefore, I was called upon to prepare Christmas dinner. While shopping for the necessities I kept thinking how un-Christmas-like the weather seemed. Yes, the streets downtown were decorated, and the stores played Christmas carols, but the temperature hovered in the sixties and there appeared to be absolutely no hope of snow.

However, as the actual day approached everybody I came in contact with seemed to mellow. People said "Merry Christmas," donated food to the poor, shopped for presents and wrapped them. It was then that it hit me. That what I had heard all my life about Christmas being a matter of peace and good will and the feelings towards your fellow man—not presents or whether snow was on the ground—was the true sense of Christmas.

That seems to sum up the feelings that the cities of Arizona exude over the holidays. Yes, the sun shines more often than not, and it is definitely not the Currier and Ives image of horse-drawn sleighs going to Grandma's house that one sees.

But there are other delights of the holiday season including the more than 6,000 luminarias that line the trail at the Desert Botanical Garden or illuminate the way to the top of Squaw Peak in Phoenix.

Nothing seems more to separate Christmas in the Southwest from the holiday celebrations in the rest of the country than the lighting of luminarias.

As early as the seventeenth century, the Indians in the territory that was to become Arizona gathered twigs and branches together and lit bonfires at Christmas time. These "little fires" called luminarias were placed in front of the churches and pueblos and were lit both to honor the birth of Christ and to light the way for people to gather.

In the 1800's the wagon trains with supplies from the east brought small Chinese paper lanterns with them. These were placed around the fronts of houses and hung from the portals or porches.

Because these lanterns were expensive and hard to come by, some creative souls began to devise different ways to make these attractive lights. What has evolved is a small paper sack, sometimes wax-lined, with a small amount of sand or dirt in the bottom and a votive candle embedded in the sand. Often, now, the sack is actually a plastic container made to look like a sack and the votive candle is an electric light bulb.

In the predominately Hispanic neighborhoods the residents look with anticipation to "La Noche Buena"—a Spanish phrase meaning " the good night": Christmas Eve. The women make the traditional foods of the holidays—tamales, menudo (tripe stew) and buñuelos.

Neighbors, friends and relatives come to the house, gather around the nacimiento (nativity scene) and sing the ancient lullaby for the Santo Nino—"A la Rurru, Niño." Then they go to church to "la Misa del Gallo," which means "the Mass of the Rooster."

This seemingly sacriligious name for a most solemn mass has its roots in Mexican folklore. The story goes that on the night Jesus was born, the animals around the manger were dismayed because there were no human visitors to the site to observe this momentous happening. The donkey and the ox did their part to celebrate the occasion by supplying warmth to the infant with their breath.

Outside, an aging rooster flew to a high point near the humble manger and, in his own way, announced the birth of the Christ child. Then another rooster joined in. Spanish-speaking people throughout the ages have passed this tale from generation to generation. Hence, the mass is called "la Misa del Gallo" in honor of the first announcers of the coming of the Messiah.

An exhibit of antique toys, ornaments, cards and period Christmas trees makes up the annual Territorial Holidays presentation during the month of December at the John C. Fremont House, 151 So. Granada Avenue, Tucson.

Celebrating the Christmas holidays in the cities of Arizona is a unique and most rewarding experience.

Main Dishes

PROSCIUTTO GREEN CHILE FRITTATA   41

CHICKEN with MANGOES and AVOCADO   42

TURKEY BREAST   43
with Curry Sauce

SOUR CREAM ENCHILADAS   44

CHICKEN FAJITAS   45

MUSHROOM SPINACH STRUDEL   46 †

HOLIDAY ROAST CHICKEN DINNER   47

FILET OF SOLE A L'ORANGE   48

TURKEY MEATBALLS with PEPPERS   49

FESTIVE VEGETARIAN LASAGNA   50

PRESCOTT QUICHE   51

CHRISTMAS HAM WITH MANGOES   52
Champagne Sauce

CHILE RELLENO CASSEROLE   53

RICE and SOUR CREAM CASSEROLE   54

BRAVA BEAN TOSTADAS   54

BLACK BEAN and CHORIZO BURRITOS   55

SCOTTSDALE EGGS   56

GREEN CORN TAMALE CASSEROLE   57

Prosciutto &
Green Chile Frittata

This makes an excellent start to a festive Christmas morning or use it as one of your dishes for a Christmas Eve buffet.

8 EGGS or the equivalent egg substitute
1 Tbsp. TEQUILA
2 Tbsp. OLIVE OIL
1/2 medium size yellow ONION, chopped
1/2 tsp. ground BLACK PEPPER
1/3 cup PROSCIUTTO or ham, shredded
1 Tbsp. PARSLEY, chopped
2 Tbsp. BUTTER
1/2 cup ripe TOMATO, chopped
1/2 cup GREEN BELL PEPPER, chopped
1/4 cup GREEN CHILE, diced
1/2 cup FETA CHEESE, crumbled
1 Tbsp. ROMANO CHEESE, grated
SOUR CREAM
chopped BLACK OLIVES

Beat the eggs with a wire whisk. Add the tequila and beat again. Heat the olive oil in a large, heavy non-stick frying pan. Cook the onion and green pepper until just soft, stir in the prosciutto, parsley and black pepper and warm through. Add the butter to the pan, and pour in the eggs. Sprinkle the tomato, chile, and the cheeses over the eggs, cover pan, and cook over very low heat for 20 minutes or until the eggs are nicely set. Cut into quarters and serve garnished with a dollop of sour cream, sprinkled with chopped black olives.

Serves 4.

Chicken with Mangoes and Avocados

Food often provides a sense of place. Avocados and mangoes always remind me of Christmas in Arizona. In combination with chicken breasts, they make an easy but memorable Christmas luncheon.

3 **Tbsp. BUTTER**
3 **Tbsp. OLIVE OIL**
4 **medium size GREEN ONIONS, chopped**
4 **CHICKEN BREASTS, boneless and skinless**
1/3 **cup DRY WHITE WINE, at room temperature**
1 **cup CREAM or HALF AND HALF**
1/2 **tsp. SALT**
1/4 **tsp. ground WHITE PEPPER**
1 **Tbsp. fresh PARSLEY, chopped**
2 **MANGOES, peeled and coarsely chopped**
2 **medium size AVOCADOS, peeled and sliced**
1 **Tbsp. LEMON JUICE**

Melt the butter in a large, heavy frying pan. Add the olive oil and let heat for a minute. Stir in the onions and cook for 2 - 3 minutes over medium heat. Saute the chicken breasts for 10 to 15 minutes or until done and lightly browned. Remove the chicken to a warm plate and keep warm. Deglaze the pan by stirring in the white wine, add the cream, salt, pepper and parsley and cook, over high heat, stirring constantly until mixture is reduced slightly (3 - 4 minutes). Stir in mangoes, reduce heat and cook, stirring a couple of times for 3 - 4 minutes or until the fruit is warmed through.

Spoon the fruit sauce over the warm chicken. Sprinkle the lemon juice over the avocado slices and arrange over the chicken.

Serves 4.

Turkey Breast with Curry Sauce

This is a great way to use that leftover holiday turkey.

16 slices TURKEY BREAST, cooked
1/2 cup CHICKEN STOCK

Arrange the turkey slices in a shallow pan, pour the chicken stock over them and warm in a 275 degree oven while making the following sauce.

Curry Sauce

1 pkg. (8 oz.) CREAM CHEESE
3 Tbsp. DRY WHITE WINE
2 tsp. LEMON JUICE
1 cup SOUR CREAM
1 tsp. CURRY POWDER
1/2 cup SLIVERED ALMONDS

Cut the cream cheese into cubes and put into a saucepan with the wine, lemon juice and sour cream and stir, over low heat, until smooth (add more liquid if necessary). Stir in the curry powder and pour over the warmed slices of turkey, sprinkle with the almonds and serve.

Serves 8.

Sour Cream Enchiladas

Friends of ours who live in Chandler invite us every year for their annual holiday bash. This traditional enchilada is always the hit of the party.

1 1/2 lbs. GROUND BEEF
1 ONION, chopped
1 clove GARLIC, minced
1/2 tsp. ground CUMIN
1/2 tsp. ground BLACK PEPPER
1/2 tsp. ground OREGANO
1 tsp. fresh CILANTRO, chopped
1/2 cup CHEDDAR CHEESE, grated
1/2 cup MONTEREY JACK CHEESE, grated
12 CORN TORTILLAS
2 cups SOUR CREAM
1 can (10 1/2 oz.) CREAM OF MUSHROOM SOUP
1 can (10 1/2 oz.) CREAM OF CELERY SOUP
1/2 cup MILK
1/2 cup GREEN CHILE, chopped
CHEDDAR CHEESE

Brown the ground beef and onion with the garlic, cumin, pepper, oregano and cilantro until the beef is brown and crumbly. Remove from the heat and stir in the cheeses. Using tongs, dip each tortilla in a frying pan with about 1/2 inch of oil and heat until soft. Spoon the filling equally among the tortillas, roll them up and place with the seam side down in a lightly greased casserole baking dish. Mix the sour cream, soups, milk and green chile together. Pour over the tortillas, sprinkle with cheddar cheese and bake in a 325 degree oven for 30 minutes or until hot and bubbly.

Serves 6 - 8.

Chicken Fajitas

This is an excellent way to feed a hungry holiday crowd. You can double or quadruple the recipe with no problems.

1 lb. BONELESS, SKINLESS CHICKEN BREASTS,
  cut in 1" x 1-1/2" strips
1/4 cup ITALIAN SALAD DRESSING
1/4 cup chopped CILANTRO
1 Tbsp. LEMON JUICE
1 clove GARLIC, minced
3 Tbsp. OLIVE OIL
2 GREEN BELL PEPPERS, cut into strips
1 RED BELL PEPPER, cut into strips
1 ONION, sliced
SOUR CREAM
GRATED CHEDDAR CHEESE
GUACAMOLE
JALAPEÑOS
SALSA
SWEET PEPPERS
WARMED FLOUR TORTILLAS

Put chicken strips in bowl, cover with Italian dressing, cilantro, lemon juice, and garlic and marinate for at least 4 hours. Cook the peppers and onion in the olive oil until limp.

Drain the chicken and grill over hot coals or cook in olive oil in a frying pan. Stir the hot chicken into the hot peppers and onions and serve with: sour cream, grated cheddar cheese, guacamole, jalapeños, salsa, sweet peppers and warmed flour tortillas.

Serves 4.

Mushroom Spinach Strudel

My German friends who lived in the Yorktown section of New York decided to chuck the high world of finance and move to Payson, Arizona. This is where they taught me how to make great, sweet holiday strudels. But as usual, I couldn't leave well enough alone and started experimenting with strudels that we could use during the Christmas season as main dishes. Served with a fruit salad, this strudel makes an elegant holiday luncheon meal.

3 Tbsp. OLIVE OIL
1 clove GARLIC, minced
1/2 ONION, chopped
1/4 cup RED BELL PEPPER, chopped
1/2 pound SPINACH, washed and torn into small pieces
1 Tbsp. MARGARINE
1 sheet PUFF PASTRY
1/4 pound MUSHROOMS, washed and sliced
1/4 cup SWISS CHEESE, shredded
1/2 tsp. SALT
1/2 tsp. ground WHITE PEPPER
1/4 tsp. ground NUTMEG

Pour 2 tablespoons of the oil into a frying pan and saute the garlic, onion and red bell pepper until limp. Stir in the spinach and continue to cook, over low heat, until the spinach is just wilted. Pour the remaining olive oil into a separate frying pan, add the margarine and saute the mushrooms until soft.

Place the puff pastry on a non-stick cookie sheet and spread the spinach mixture down the center of the pastry the long way. Top with the mushrooms, sprinkle with the cheese, salt, pepper and nutmeg. Lift one side of the dough over the vegetables, then lift the other side of the dough to overlap the first. Bake in a 375 degree oven for 20 minutes or until the pastry is nicely browned. Slice and serve warm.

4 luncheon size servings.

Holiday Roast Chicken Dinner

3 to 3 1/2 lbs. CHICKEN
WATER
1 Tbsp. COARSE (Kosher) SALT
1/4 cup OLIVE OIL
1 tsp. ground PAPRIKA
1 cup dry WHITE WINE
1 cup WATER
1 CLOVE GARLIC, minced
1 tsp. ground SAGE
1 Tbsp. fresh PARSLEY, chopped
1/2 tsp. ground WHITE PEPPER
4 medium size CARROTS, sliced
3 medium size POTATOES, peeled
    and quartered
8 small ONIONS, peeled (or 4
    medium size onions)
1/4 cup DRY WHITE WINE
2 Tbsp. BRANDY

Soak the chicken in water to cover with the coarse salt for 1/2 hour. Drain and rinse under cold running water. Pat dry with paper towel. Place chicken in roasting pan and rub with olive oil. Sprinkle paprika over top of chicken. Mix together the wine, water, garlic, sage, parsley, and pepper and pour into the bottom of the roasting pan. Bake, covered, in a preheated 450 degree oven for 10 minutes. Remove the cover, add the carrots, potatoes and onions, reduce the heat to 350 and cook for 35 - 45 more minutes or until the chicken and vegetables are done, adding more water if necessary.

When done, remove chicken to a warm serving plate or platter, and arrange the vegetables around it.

Deglaze the roasting pan with the additional 1/4 cup white wine and the brandy and serve on the side with the chicken.

Serves 4.

Filet of Sole a L'Orange

This wonderfully delicate fish dish makes a great holiday offering either on a buffet or for a special luncheon. You can substitute Pollack or any other tender white fish filets, if you wish.

1 1/2 to 2 lbs. FILET OF SOLE or other WHITE FISH
1 1/2 cups CHICKEN BROTH
3 medium size GREEN ONIONS, chopped
1 Tbsp. fresh PARSLEY, chopped
1 tsp. CORNSTARCH
1/2 cup FRESH ORANGE JUICE
1 Tbsp. ORANGE FLAVORED LIQUEUR
1 tsp. ORANGE PEEL
ORANGE SLICES
CILANTRO SPRIGS

Arrange the filets in a microwave-safe cooking dish. Pour 1/2 cup of the chicken broth over the fish, sprinkle the onions and parsley on top, cover with plastic wrap and cook in the microwave, on high for 6 - 8 minutes or until fish tests done when tested with a fork. While the fish is cooking, dissolve the cornstarch in the orange juice in a saucepan. Add the additional 1 cup of chicken broth. Stir in the orange liqueur and orange peel and cook over medium heat until sauce has thickened.

Remove the fish from the microwave, drain off the liquid and arrange on warm plates or serving platter. Spoon the orange sauce over the fish, arrange orange slices and cilantro around the fish and serve.

Serves 4.

Turkey Meatballs with Peppers

Who doesn't have left-over turkey during the holidays? This is one great way to use up some of that bird.

1 lb. TURKEY, cooked, ground
1 medium size ONION, chopped
1/2 cup DRY BREAD CRUMBS
1/2 tsp. SALT
1/2 tsp. GROUND BLACK PEPPER
1 tsp. RED CHILE POWDER
1 tsp. DRIED PARSLEY, crushed
1/2 tsp. CUMIN
2 EGGS, beaten
2 Tbsp. BUTTER or MARGARINE
3 Tbsp. OLIVE OIL

Mix all the ingredients, <u>except</u> butter and oil, together and shape into balls the size of large walnuts. Saute in the butter and olive oil, moving gently with a slotted spoon until browned on all sides. While they are cooking, prepare the following:

2 Tbsp. BUTTER or MARGARINE
2 Tbsp. OLIVE OIL
2 medium size GREEN BELL PEPPERS, cut into strips
1 medium size RED BELL PEPPER, cut into strips
1 large ONION, thinly sliced
1 cup CURRANT JELLY
2 Tbsp. LEMON JUICE
1 Tbsp. ORANGE PEEL, grated
1 tsp. RED CHILE POWDER
1 cup TOMATO SAUCE

Saute the bell peppers and onions in the butter and olive oil until just limp. Stir in the rest of the ingredients and cook a few minutes. Stir in cooked meatballs, let cook 2 - 3 more minutes before serving.

Serves 4.

Festive Vegetarian Lasagna

If any family members or friends are vegetarians, this makes a nice holiday dish for them or a super addition to a buffet.

10 oz. LASAGNA NOODLES
WATER to cover
2 Tbsp. OLIVE OIL
1/2 medium size YELLOW ONION, finely chopped
1 CLOVE GARLIC, finely minced
1 Tbsp. fresh PARSLEY, finely chopped
1/2 Tbsp. fresh CILANTRO, finely chopped
1/2 tsp. SALT
1/2 tsp. ground BLACK PEPPER
1 Tbsp. BASIL, chopped (or 1/2 tsp. dried basil)
1/2 tsp. dried OREGANO
1/4 tsp. NUTMEG
2 EGGS (can use egg substitute)
1 carton (15 oz.) of RICOTTA CHEESE
1/2 cup cooked, diced TURNIP GREENS, squeezed dry
1/2 cup cooked, diced FRESH SPINACH, squeezed dry
1 can (28 oz.) whole, peeled cooked TOMATOES
1/4 cup SALSA or TACO SAUCE
1 cup diced, cooked ZUCCHINI
1/4 cup chopped BLACK OLIVES
1/4 cup grated SWISS or MOZZARELLA CHEESE
1/4 cup grated CHEDDAR CHEESE
2 Tbsp. grated ROMANO CHEESE

Cook the lasagna noodles in boiling water until just soft (about 10 minutes), and drain. Heat the oil in a frying pan and saute the onion and garlic until they start to soften. Stir in the parsley, cilantro, salt, pepper, basil, oregano, and nutmeg. Cook until the parsley and cilantro are wilted.

Beat the eggs in a small bowl and then beat the ricotta cheese into the eggs, a little at a time, with a fork. Put the tomatoes with the juice and the taco salsa in a blender and puree. Layer the bottom of a lightly greased 9 x 13 inch baking pan with a layer of the noodles, making sure the pieces overlap. Spread half of the ricotta and egg mixture on the noodles, then layer half the greens, cheese, zucchini and olives. Top with half of the tomato mixture. Repeat the process. Top with the Romano cheese and bake in a 350 degree oven for 45 minutes or until heated through and bubbly.

Serves 4.

Prescott Quiche

Preheat oven to 400 degrees

1 Tbsp. OLIVE OIL
1/2 cup sliced or chopped fresh MUSHROOMS
1/4 cup ONION, finely chopped
1 cup finely chopped, COOKED GREENS (we
    use a mixture of collard greens and
    mustard greens but you can substitute
    turnip greens or Swiss chard or spinach)
1/2 cup SWISS CHEESE, finely chopped
1/4 cup chopped, COOKED HAM (may omit for
    a vegetarian quiche)
1/4 cup chopped BLACK OLIVES
2 Tbsp. fresh PARSLEY, finely chopped
1/2 tsp. SALT
1/2 tsp. GROUND BLACK PEPPER
3 EGGS
1 cup MILK or half and half
1 UNBAKED 9-inch DEEP DISH PIE CRUST

Saute the onions and mushrooms in the olive oil until soft. Drain and reserve. Spread the greens evenly in the bottom of the pie crust. Spoon the mushrooms and onions over the greens. Sprinkle the ham, olives, cheese and the seasonings over the vegetables.

Beat the eggs, and then beat the milk into them (I find using a blender for this operation works great). Pour the egg mixture over the quiche filling. Use a spoon and make sure the egg and milk mixture flows to the bottom of the pan. Set the pan on a cookie sheet and bake in a 400 degree oven for 15 minutes. Reduce the heat to 350 degrees and continue to bake for 30 more minutes or until the quiche is a golden brown on top and firm in the center.

Serves 4.

Christmas Ham with Mangoes

We particularly like to have ham for New Year's and have spent years trying different recipes. This recipe evolved over a couple of years. We feel it is the best ever, and will remain our standard ham recipe for many years to come.

1/2 HAM, butt portion (approximately 8 pounds)
WHOLE CLOVES

Score the fat side of the ham with a knife making a checkerboard pattern. Insert whole cloves into each intersection of the cuts.

Place the ham in a roasting pan and prepare the following mixture to pour over the ham.

1 cup SLICED MANGOES (if possible fresh mangoes sold
in glass jars in the produce section of the
supermarket), drained. Reserve the juice.
1 cup MANGO JUICE
2 Tbsp. MOLASSES
1 Tbsp. GRAND MARNIER (or other orange-flavored
liqueur)
1 tsp. ground GINGER
1 tsp. ground CLOVES
1 Tbsp. ORANGE MARMALADE
1 tsp. DRY MUSTARD

Put all the ingredients into a blender and blend until smooth. Pour over the ham, letting the mixture slowly slide down the front of the ham into the baking pan.

Next, carefully stir 1/2 to 1 cup water into the mango mixture in the pan. Bake the ham in a 350 degree oven for 2 to 2 1/2 hours, basting several times during the baking. Add additional water to the pan juices if they are getting too thick or threaten to stick to the bottom of the pan.

When the ham is done, remove to a cutting board and pour the pan juices into a saucepan. Use a little hot water to deglaze the pan. Add this to the saucepan and place over low heat.

Continued next page . . .

Continued from previous page . . .

Champagne Sauce

2 Tbsp. CORNSTARCH
1/4 cup COLD WATER
1/2 cup DRY or BRUT CHAMPAGNE

Dissolve cornstarch in the cold water, stir into mango sauce and cook until it starts to thicken. Then stir in champagne and cook until sauce has thickened to spoonable consistency. Slice the ham and serve with warm sauce on the side.

Serves 8 - 10.

Chile Relleno Casserole

Angie Garcia of Tucson gave me this particularly nice and very easy to prepare dish. It can be a great side dish or a vegetarian meal for green chile lovers. Make it in advance and you'll have plenty of time for your guests!

12 GREEN CHILES, seeded and sliced into quarters
2 cups MONTEREY JACK CHEESE, shredded
4 EGG YOLKS, lightly beaten
1/2 tsp. SALT
1 clove GARLIC, minced
1/4 tsp. CAYENNE PEPPER
3 Tbsp. ALL-PURPOSE FLOUR
1/2 cup EVAPORATED MILK
4 EGG WHITES, stiffly beaten

Layer chiles and cheese, alternately in a 9 x 13 inch glass casserole dish. Mix together the egg yolks, salt, garlic, cayenne, flour and milk. Fold the egg whites into the mixture and pour over the chile and cheese layers. Bake in a 325 degree oven for 1 hour.

Serves 8 - 10.

Rice and Sour Cream Casserole

For a change from potatoes, try this wonderful combination of flavors with your holiday goose or turkey.

2 cups SOUR CREAM	1 Tbsp. PARSLEY, chopped
3 cups cooked RICE	1 cup MONTEREY JACK
1 cup GREEN CHILE, chopped	CHEESE, grated
1 tsp. SALT	1 cup CHEDDAR CHEESE, grated
1 tsp. ground BLACK PEPPER	

Mix the sour cream, rice, chile, salt, pepper and parsley together. Spoon 1/2 of the mixture into a lightly greased casserole dish. Mix the 2 cheeses together and sprinkle half of the cheese over the rice mixture. Top with the rest of the rice, then top with the remainder of the cheese. Bake in a 350 degree oven for 30 minutes.

Serves 8 - 10.

Brava Bean Tostadas

One Christmas season we attended a musical offering in Phoenix. In a fit of stage passion the zaftig soprano threw herself on the floor and after several attempts by the tenor to get her to her feet proved futile she bravely finished her aria in a prone position, resting her head on her arm.

She so delighted the audience that the "bravas" were almost deafening so we thought it fitting to name this appetizer in remembrance of that gutsy lady and her wonderful performance.

12 slices BACON	TACO SAUCE
1 cup GREEN BELL PEPPERS, sliced	1 head LETTUCE, shredded
12 TOSTADA SHELLS	1 cup MONTEREY JACK or CHEDDAR CHEESE
1 can (16 oz.) REFRIED BEANS	1 cup TOMATOES diced

Fry bacon until crisp; drain on paper towels and crumble. In the drippings, saute bell peppers until crisp-tender. Spread shells evenly with refried beans; spoon 1 tablespoon taco sauce over beans. Spoon bell pepper and bacon on top. Sprinkle with lettuce, cheese and tomatoes and serve.

Serves 6.

Black Bean & Chorizo Burritos

This is nice for a holiday brunch, to eat in front of the TV on New Year's day or serve to the crowd after a U of A vs. ASU game.

3 **Tbsp. OLIVE OIL**
2 **CLOVES GARLIC, minced**
1 **medium size ONION, chopped**
1 **GREEN BELL PEPPER, chopped**
1 **lb. CHORIZO**
2 **cups COOKED BLACK BEANS (drained or canned)**
1/2 **cup GREEN CHILE, chopped**
1 **JALAPENO, seeded and chopped**
8 **large FLOUR TORTILLAS**
SOUR CREAM
SLICED BLACK OLIVES

Saute the garlic, onion and green bell pepper in the olive oil, then crumble the chorizo in the pan and brown the meat. Drain off any excess fat. Mash the beans and stir them into the pan along with the green chile and jalapeno and cook over low heat until the beans are warm. Warm the tortillas, one at a time, in a frying pan or microwave.

Spoon two tablespoons of the bean and meat mixture along the center of each tortilla, roll up and fold in the ends. Serve with dollop of sour cream and garnish with black olives.

Serves 4.

Scottsdale Eggs

1 cup VELVEETA®, cubed
1/4 cup GREEN CHILE, chopped
1/3 cup EVAPORATED MILK
1 clove GARLIC, run through a garlic press
pinch CAYENNE PEPPER
LETTUCE
8 pieces of LIGHTLY BUTTERED TOAST
8 POACHED EGGS
slices of JALAPENOS

Melt the Velveeta in a microwave. Stir in the green chile, milk, garlic and cayenne (add more milk if necessary to make a smooth sauce.) Place two lettuce leaves on a plate for each serving. Top with two pieces of toast. Top the toast with eggs, pour the cheese sauce over the eggs, garnish with a slice of jalapeno and serve.

Serves 4.

Green Corn Tamale Casserole

Lots of people living in Arizona do not feel it is Christmas without tamales. As they can be extremely time consuming and difficult to make, you may want to try this casserole for the same taste sensation and a lot less work.

2 Tbsp. OLIVE OIL
1 yellow ONION, diced
1 can (16 oz.) WHOLE KERNEL CORN, drained
1/2 cup GREEN CHILE, diced
1 clove GARLIC, minced
2 Tbsp. BUTTER
2 Tbsp. ALL-PURPOSE FLOUR
2 cups MILK
1 Tbsp. CILANTRO, chopped
1/2 tsp. SALT
1/2 tsp. CUMIN
1 tsp. ground BLACK PEPPER
3 EGGS, lightly beaten
8 CORN TORTILLAS, cut into strips
1 cup COLBY CHEESE, shredded

Saute the onion in the olive oil. Add the corn, chile and garlic. In another frying pan make a roux using the butter and flour. Add the milk and stir until smooth. Stir in the corn/chili mixture. Add the cilantro, salt, cumin and pepper and stir. Then add in the eggs. Grease a 9 x 13 inch glass casserole dish and layer half of the tortilla strips on the bottom of the dish. Spoon half of the corn/chili mixture on top of them. Layer the rest of the tortilla strips and top with the rest of the corn/chili mixture. Top with the cheese and bake in 350 degree oven for 30 - 40 minutes or until nicely browned on top.

Serves 4 - 6.

Tucson, Arizona

Arizona Daily Star

December 25, 1912

DOMESTIC SCIENCE DEPARTMENT

Conducted by

Mrs. Alice Gitchell Kirk

The demand for chafing dishes has grown to very large proportions and there are good reasons for this. The convenience of the chafing dish, the palatableness of the dishes produced, everything hot and right from the fire to the plate; the opportunity for showing one's grace and ability in cooking and serving, the possibilities of little experiments and changes in conditions, the personality and interest attaching to the actual culinary operations, all these combine to make the chafing dish a favorite utensil in every family. It is generally looked upon as a luxury and its use a passing fad.

Where welsh rarebit, lobsters or crabs are served, avoid a heavy sweet at the end.

Welsh Rarebit

Materials - American cheese (yellow) one pound; butter, one tablespoonful; catsup, one tablespoonful; ale or beer, one-half cup; salt, one-half teaspoonful; horse radish, one-half teaspoonful; clove of garlic, one; cayenne pepper, Worcestershire sauce.

Utensils - Chafing dish, grater, tablespoon, teaspoon.

Directions - Grate the cheese or cut it very fine. Rub the pan with the garlic. Mix all the seasonings with the cheese. Heat the beer and, when boiling hot, add the cheese mixture and stir rapidly and constantly until smooth and creamy. Beat very hard at the last and serve at once on squares of toast.

Be very sure the plates are very hot, also the toast, and ready the instant the rarebit is done. The success of this depends largely upon the cheese. Good English dairy cheese makes a good rarebit. Do not cook after the cheese is well melted, as it is apt to separate. A beaten yolk or two of egg added at the last, some think, is an improvement.

CHAPTER FOUR

Celebrating Christmas Arizona Style

The celebration of Christmas takes many forms as you travel around the state of Arizona.

In Willcox they kick off the holiday season the first week of December with a Christmas Apple Festival. There is a bazaar chock full of arts and crafts and they hold a cooking contest.

Yuma has a long history of Christian celebrations dating from 1540. Seventy years before Jamestown was founded, the Spanish conquistadores and missionaries crossed the Colorado River at the Yuma crossing.

In 1780 Father Francisco Garces founded the Las Puisima Concepcion Mission on the site that became Fort Yuma and ministered to the Indians teaching them the glories of Christ and his birth.

Spanish settlers followed Father Kino into Tubac in the early eighteenth century. Set between San Xavier and Tumacacori, Tubac periodically had a turbulent past. Ruins of the presidio or fort that housed the Spanish garrison still remain. In the mid 1800's gold and silver was mined northwest and east of Tubac in the Santa Rita mountains. Both Papagos (Tohono O'odham) and workers from Mexico traded salt and vegetables to the miners and Tubac prospered for a time.

An account of a resident of the time tells of a Christmas dinner of bear and other wild game for twenty people. It was topped off by wine brought in on the wagon trains and carols played slightly off key by a Mexican guitarist.

In the middle of December Tubac now celebrates the holiday with the Fiesta Navidad & The Festival of Lights complete with luminarias and carolers.

Los Pastores has been one of the historic ways that the people of Mexican and Spanish descent have celebrated Christmas.

Los Pastores are religious folk plays dating from medieval times. These centuries-old dramas were brought from Spain to Mexico by the Franciscan monks, probably to explain the story of Christmas to the Indians.

The plays then found their way to Arizona and continued being performed throughout the territory until the early twentieth century. Although they are infrequently performed today many of the older generation still remember their charm. Traditionally, Los Pastores were not written down but verbally handed from one generation to another.

The story is a simple one. The play opens with the devil, in the form of Lucifer, grotesquely made up. He is furious at Isaiah's prophecy of the coming of a savior. Other actors dressed as "diablitos," or little devils dance around in a parody of evil wrath.

Next a group of shepherds tending their flocks see the brilliant winter star announcing the birth of Christ.

In order to welcome the Savior, they embark on their journey to Bethlehem. Although he protests all the way, they drag along the drunken shepherd, Bartolo. While the other shepherds offer gifts and sing the praises of the Christ child, Bartolo drinks and nods off. However, upon seeing the baby Jesus, Bartolo casts off his life of sin and debauchery and offers his life to the service of Christ.

At the conclusion of the play everyone rejoices and the actors sing "Noche Buena, Noche Santa" (Silent Night). The audience joins in as the play comes to an end. Then the members of the cast and audience gather for refreshments.

The portrayal of the clash between good and evil, the costuming, humor, singing, camaraderie, good food, and good cheer all contribute in making Los Pastores a fond memory of an Arizona Christmas.

* * *

The strikingly modern Chapel of Holy Cross set in a base of pinnacled rock and framed by the imposing red rock mountain that curves around the back of it illustrates the "spirituality" of Sedona.

A mecca for followers of the New Age movement, Sedona is without a doubt one of the most beautiful spots on earth and annually hosts over two million tourists. Every year the town is awash in the Christmas spirit during the holidays and the many art galleries, crafts shops and restaurants are decorated for the season.

* * *

It snows enough in and around Flagstaff so that nearby Fairfield Snow Bowl is a popular ski resort. The majestic San Francisco mountains are the highest in Arizona and are capped with snow during the holiday season.

The pine trees that surround the city remind one of how Flagstaff got its name; in 1876 pioneers who arrived on July 4th stripped a pine tree and used it as a flagpole to celebrate the one hundredth anniversary of the signing of the Declaration of Independence.

While eating in the Weatherford Hotel built at the turn-of-the-century, one can imagine the elaborate Christmas dinners of a bygone era once served there.

Whether in the northern or southern parts of the state, with or without snow, on the east side or west side.

Christmas is a very special time and is a cherished memory for the people who live in and visit Arizona.

ANGEL

STORYTELLER

SAN PASQUAL
The patron Saint of kitchens

Folk art representation of
one of the manger animals

(Photos by Author)

Side Dishes

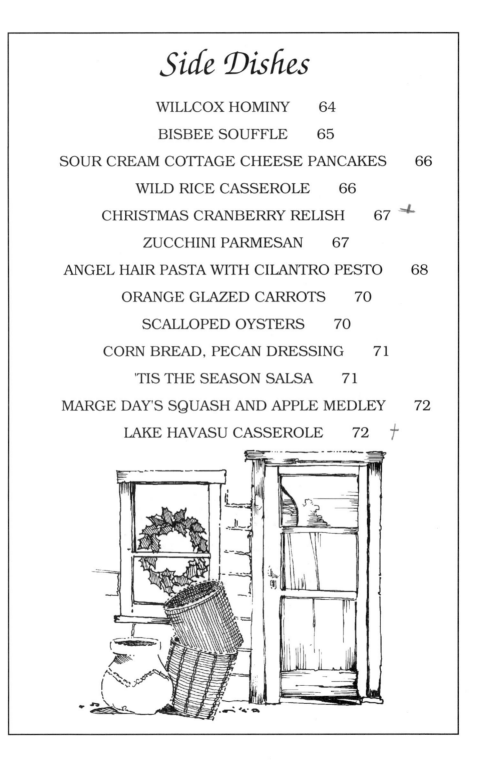

Willcox Hominy

1   can (30 oz.) HOMINY
1   cup COLBY CHEESE, grated
1   large ONION, chopped
1   cup GREEN CHILE, chopped
2   Tbsp. BUTTER or MARGARINE
2   Tbsp. ALL-PURPOSE FLOUR
2   cups MILK
1   clove GARLIC, minced
1   tsp. OREGANO
1   tsp. CUMIN
1   tsp. SALT
1   tsp. RED CHILE POWDER

Drain hominy. Place alternate layers of hominy, cheese, onion and green chile in a well-greased 9 x 13 inch baking pan. Make a roux with the butter and flour, stir in the milk. Add garlic, oregano, cumin, salt and red chile powder. Pour over hominy mixture and bake at 350 degrees for 1 hour.

Serves 6 - 8.

Bisbee Souffle

An old-timer told me the story, most likely apocryphal, that this dish was served to Teddy Roosevelt on one of his visits to the Copper Queen Hotel in Bisbee.

2 Tbsp. BUTTER
2 Tbsp. ALL-PURPOSE FLOUR
1 1/4 cups MILK
1/2 cup LONGHORN CHEESE, grated
1 cup COOKED CORN
1/2 cup GREEN CHILE, chopped
2 Tbsp. PIMENTO, chopped
1/2 tsp. CUMIN
1/2 tsp. SALT
1/2 tsp. ground WHITE PEPPER
dash TABASCO® sauce
3 EGGS, separated
1/2 tsp. CREAM OF TARTAR

Melt the butter in a frying pan. Stir in the flour, then the milk and cook for 4 - 5 minutes, stirring constantly. Stir in the cheese, corn, chile, pimento, cumin, salt, pepper and Tabasco. Remove from heat and let cool slightly. Beat the egg yolks and then stir into the mixture, blending well. Beat the egg whites until they start to stiffen, add the cream of tartar to them and beat until stiff. Fold the egg whites into the cheese and corn mixture and pour into an ungreased 1 1/2 quart souffle dish. Bake for 30 minutes in a 350 degree oven. Serve immediately.

Serves 4 - 6.

Sour Cream Cottage Cheese Pancakes

Everyone will look forward to this wonderfully elegant pancake!

3/4 cup SOUR CREAM
2 EGGS
1/2 cup COTTAGE CHEESE
1/2 cup ALL-PURPOSE FLOUR

2 tsp. BAKING POWDER
1/2 tsp. SALT
1/4 tsp. ground NUTMEG

Put all the ingredients into a blender and blend until smooth. Lightly grease a griddle and heat. Cook the pancakes until lightly browned on both sides and serve with orange marmalade or fruit preserves.

Makes approximately 8 pancakes.

Wild Rice Casserole

We know some "snowbirds" from Minnesota who winter in Yuma. They always bring wild rice with them and this recipe is their contribution to the annual Holiday potluck dinner at their RV park.

3 Tbsp. BUTTER
3 Tbsp. OLIVE OIL
1 medium size ONION, chopped
2 cups WILD RICE
4 1/2 cups CHICKEN BROTH
1 cup FRESH MUSHROOMS, sliced

1/2 cup SLIVERED ALMONDS
1/2 tsp. SAFFLOWER
1 tsp. PARSLEY, chopped
1 clove GARLIC, minced
1/2 tsp. ROSEMARY, crushed

Heat the butter and oil in a frying pan, and saute the onion until soft. Stir in the rice and coat with the oil and butter. Mix with the rest of the ingredients and put into a lightly greased, covered casserole dish. Bake in a 325 degree oven for 1 hour. Uncover and bake for 30 more minutes or until rice is tender.

Serves 8 - 10.

Christmas Cranberry Relish

This will be a winner for the transplants from the east that <u>must</u> have their cranberries for Christmas.

1 can (16 oz.) WHOLE CRANBERRY SAUCE
1/4 cup ORANGE JUICE
1 tsp. grated ORANGE PEEL
1/2 cup RAISINS
1/2 cup SLIVERED ALMONDS, chopped
1/2 cup WALNUTS, chopped
1/4 tsp. ground CINNAMON
1/4 tsp. ground NUTMEG
1 Tbsp. BRANDY

Mix all the ingredients together and chill in the refrigerator before serving.

Serves 6 - 8.

Zucchini Parmesan

Squash has been a long-time staple of the native American diet. This recipe makes a great accompaniment to a Christmas roast.

1/4 cup BUTTER
2 Tbsp. OLIVE OIL
1/4 cup YELLOW ONION, finely chopped
1 clove GARLIC, minced
2 cups ZUCCHINI, sliced
1/2 tsp. SALT
1/2 tsp. GROUND BLACK PEPPER
1/4 cup PARMESAN CHEESE

Melt the butter in a large frying pan. Add the olive oil, then stir in the onion. Cook the onion and garlic for 2 - 3 minutes, then add the zucchini, salt and pepper. Cook uncovered over low heat for 10 minutes. Cover and cook for 5 more minutes or until the zucchini is done to taste. Toss with the Parmesan cheese over medium heat for 1 - 2 minutes and serve immediately.

Serves 4.

Angel Hair Pasta with Cilantro Pesto

THE PESTO:

1/2 cup fresh CILANTRO
1/2 cup fresh PARSLEY
1 clove GARLIC, chopped
1/4 cup ROMANO CHEESE, grated
3 Tbsp. chopped PECANS
1 tsp. fresh LIME JUICE
1/4 tsp. SALT
1/2 tsp. COARSELY GROUND BLACK PEPPER
1/4 cup OLIVE OIL

Coarsely chop the cilantro and parsley and then put into a blender along with the garlic, cheese, pecans, lime juice, salt and pepper. Slowly add the olive oil and blend until the pesto is smooth. If the mixture is too thick add more olive oil.

Makes approximately 1 cup

THE PASTA:

12 ounces ANGEL HAIR PASTA
1/2 tsp. COARSE (Kosher) SALT
1 tsp. OLIVE OIL

Cook pasta in boiling water, with the salt and olive oil for 7 - 8 minutes or until done to taste. Drain and then mix with the sauce.

THE SAUCE:

1/4 lb. BUTTER
2 Tbsp. OLIVE OIL
1 Tbsp. CILANTRO PESTO (add more to taste, if desired)
FRESHLY GRATED ROMANO CHEESE
DRIED ITALIAN RED PEPPER FLAKES

While the pasta is cooking, melt the butter in a large frying pan, add the olive oil and the pesto. When hot, toss the angel hair into the pan and let heat for just a few seconds. Serve topped with freshly grated Romano cheese and a sprinkle of red pepper flakes, if desired.

Serves 4.

Is There a Santa Claus?

Is there a Santa Claus?
You with the truth in your eyes,
Bidding one ponder and pause,
You that sift truth from the lies,
You that with faith in your heart
Clamber at night on my knee . . .

If you belive there is -
I, and you know it is true!
Truly, that spirit is his
Throbbing with kindness to you.
Truly, that influence deep
That goes the warmth of your smile,
Blesses your dreams when you sleep,
Stays with you all of the while.

I have no casuist's art;
Truly, the Saint used to be!

Is there a Santa Claus?
You ask again and again,
Now must I answer, because
You have the trust I had then.
You have the trusting belief
That once my spirit possesed
Ere there came worry and grief
Biding their while in my breast

Listen!   Is there an arm
Holding you close to my heart,
Fending you ever from harm
Holding the darkness apart
Is there a spirit of love
Waiting with wings ever spread
Beside you, about you, above,
And warding wherever you're led?

Is there a Santa Claus?
Yes!   Little one with your eyes
Bidding me ponder and pause
Ere I tell you that are wise.
Shatter the faith that you hold?
Give you a pang of distress?
Yes, for the young and the old
There is a Santa Claus.   Yes!

Arizona Daily Star
Tucson, Arizona
December 19, 1912

Orange Glazed Carrots

This dish is more attractive if you use baby carrots. If you can't find them, substitute large whole carrots cut into thirds or quarters.

24 SMALL CARROTS
1 tsp. DRIED MINT, crushed
3 Tbsp. BUTTER or MARGARINE
2 Tbsp. HONEY
2 Tbsp. ORANGE FLAVORED LIQUEUR
1 Tbsp. ORANGE PEEL, grated

Cook the carrots in water to cover with the mint or steam in a microwave until just tender. Melt the butter in a frying pan, stir in the honey, liqueur and orange peel and cook over low heat, stirring constantly until smooth. Drain the carrots and stir the hot carrots into the orange honey mixture until the carrots are coated. Garnish with fresh mint and serve.

Serves 4 - 6.

Scalloped Oysters

This is a "must serve" dish at Christmas time for all of the "Sons and Daughters of the South" now residing in the great state of Arizona.

2 Tbsp. BUTTER or MARGARINE
2 Tbsp. WORCESTERSHIRE SAUCE
2 Dashes TABASCO® SAUCE
1 Tbsp. LEMON JUICE
1 Tbsp. FRESH PARSLEY, chopped
2 doz. LARGE FRESH OYSTERS with the liquid
1/2 Box SALTINE CRACKERS, crushed

Melt the butter and mix with the Worcestershire Sauce, Tabasco sauce, lemon juice, parsley and the liquid from the oysters and set aside. Roll the oysters in the cracker crumbs and layer them in a lightly greased glass 9 x 9 inch baking dish, alternating with cracker crumbs. Then slowly pour the liquid over the top, dot with butter and bake for 20 - 30 minutes in a 375 degree oven.

Serve 6 - 8.

Corn Bread, Pecan Dressing

Arizona has some of the largest pecan orchards in the country and since the crop is ready in late November they are a natural for your holiday dishes.

2 Tbsp. BUTTER or MARGARINE
2 Tbsp. OLIVE OIL
1 ONION, chopped
1 stalk (or 6 ribs) CELERY, chopped
2 Tbsp. PARSLEY, chopped
3 cups CORN BREAD (Use the recipe on the package of
      corn meal)
3 cups WHITE BREAD CRUMBS
2 EGGS, lightly beaten
2 cups CHICKEN STOCK or JUICE from COOKING TURKEY
      GIBLETS
1 cup PECANS, chopped
1/2 cup PIMENTO, chopped
2 tsp. POULTRY SEASONING
1 tsp. ground BLACK PEPPER
1 tsp. SALT

Saute the onion, celery, and parsley in the butter and olive oil until soft. Crumble the cornbread into a large bowl, stir in the rest of the ingredients, then spoon into a greased glass baking dish and bake in a 350 degree oven 45 minutes to 1 hour or until the top is lightly browned.

Serves 6 - 8.

'Tis the Season Salsa

Many folks would feel absolutely deprived if they couldn't have salsa with their Christmas dinner. This simple blend of fresh vegetables makes a great addition to any holiday meal.

2 lg. FIRM RIPE TOMATOES, chopped
1 lg. WHITE ONION, chopped
2 JALAPENOS, seeded and chopped
JUICE of 2 LIMES

Mix together and refrigerate. Great served with turkey or fish.

Marge Day's Squash & Apple Medley

Mrs. Day helps with research material for our books, lends moral support and comes up with some real winning recipes like this delightful combination.

2 large ZUCCHINI, sliced
2 GRANNY SMITH APPLES, cored, sliced
1 ONION, sliced
1 clove GARLIC, minced
1/2 tsp. SALT
1/2 tsp. ground BLACK PEPPER
SALSA
MONTEREY JACK CHEESE, grated

Put all the ingredients <u>except</u> the salsa and cheese in a microwave safe bowl, cover with plastic wrap and cook on high 6 - 8 minutes or until vegetables are done. Sprinkle with cheese and serve hot with your favorite salsa on the side.

Serves 4.

Lake Havasu Casserole

4 cups MASHED POTATOES
1 cup SOUR CREAM
1 tsp. SALT
1 tsp. ground BLACK PEPPER
1/2 tsp. CAYENNE PEPPER
1 medium size ONION, chopped
1/4 cup BUTTER or MARGARINE
1 pkg. (10 ounces) FROZEN CHOPPED SPINACH, thawed
    well drained and squeezed dry
1/2 cup GREEN CHILE, chopped
1 cup COLBY CHEESE, shredded

Combine all the ingredients, <u>except</u> the cheese, in a well-greased glass baking dish. Sprinkle the cheese over the top and bake in a 350 degree oven for 20 minutes.

Serves 4 - 6.

CHAPTER FIVE

The Indians of Arizona

In the eyes of the Spaniards who found the territory that was to become Arizona, it more closely resembled the Holy Land at the time of Christ than any other place. The similarity exists to this day; palm trees, almonds, olives, and pomegranates all grow in parts of Arizona.

The Indian tribes that inhabited this land lived according to prophecies, traditions, and beliefs foreign to the Europeans. The missionary padres set out to convert the Indians to Christianity and were successful—but only to a point—as today many of the Indian tribes of Arizona practice Christian beliefs along with their age-old rites.

The various Indian tribes that have lived in Arizona include the Mohave, Chemehuevi, Papago (now called Tohono O'odham), Yuma, Cocopah, Hualpai, Paiute, Havasupai, Hopi, Navajo, Yavapai, Apache, Pima, and Maricopa.

When the Spaniards began their explorations, they discovered Hopis living on three small mesas. Legend has it the Indians had stayed on these mesas waiting for the promised return of a god. Hopi culture is rich in lore and religious heritage and the Hopis have a closely knit social order. Masked men, called kachinas, play an important role in Hopi ceremonies. There are three facets to a kachina. The first two are a supernatural being that exists in the minds of the Hopi and the masked impersonator of that being. The third is the kachina doll that takes its shape and appearance from the masked impersonators.

Just as today's children believe in Santa Claus, Hopi children believe in kachinas. Certain kachinas bring the children sweet cakes, fruit, and candies from the latter part of December through July. Most importantly, the kachina dolls given to Hopi children are not toys but objects to be studied and treasured.

To the Hopis, corn has more meaning than just food. An important part of the ceremonial and ritual life of the tribe, corn is a symbol of friendship and fertility. To ensure a good harvest, prayers are said twice a year in the hand-planted Hopi cornfields.

The corn grown by the Hopis is unlike the corn you find in the produce section of your supermarket. The ears come in an array of different colors: white, yellow, blue and red. The blue corn, which looks almost black when still on the cob is a grayish blue when turned into cornmeal. It tastes like a mixture of popcorn and hominy and is the most prevalent corn found on the Hopi reservation.

Among the dishes made from blue cornmeal are corn pudding, piki bread which is baked on a grill, blue cornmeal pancakes, posole, and blue cornmeal tortillas.

Tribes that figured prominently in Arizona's history included the Pimas who in the seventeenth century lived along the Gila River and the Papagos (Tohono O'odham) who inhabited the desert lands to the south of the Gila.

These Indian tribes were originally gatherers who later started cultivating the land and grew such crops as beans, squash, wheat, melons and corn.

After the introduction of European livestock, the Navajos raised sheep and pursued cultivation of the land. Many a Christmas dinner has been dropped by helicopter to Navajo families stranded by heavy snow on their sheep ranches in northern Arizona.

There are legends about a tribal hero who acquired such crops as beans, squash, and corn directly from the gods. The long tradition of using these foods in ancient rites is passed down to today's Christmas celebrations. Green corn tamales, beans served in a multitude of ways, and squash made into muffins, bread or served with chile, are an integral part of the wonderful holiday meals prepared and shared by Arizonans.

San Xavier del Bac, dubbed "the white dove of the desert," is located nine miles southwest of Tucson on the San Xavier Indian Reservation, the home of the Tohono O'odham. Many special religious festivities are held at San Xavier during the month of December.

Breads

Show Low Corn Bread

This is a perfect blue corn meal recipe. Blue corn has just recently become very chic with gourmets and foodies although our native Americans have been using it for centuries.

Preheat oven to 375 degrees

6 slices SLICED BACON
1 cup YELLOW or BLUE CORN MEAL
1 cup ALL-PURPOSE FLOUR
1 tsp. BAKING SODA
3 tsp. BAKING POWDER
2 EGGS, slightly beaten
1 1/4 cups BUTTERMILK
1/4 cup VEGETABLE OIL
4 oz. GREEN CHILE, chopped

Cook bacon until crisp in a cast-iron skillet. Remove from the skillet and reserve the drippings. Crumble the bacon and reserve. Put the skillet, with drippings, in the oven to heat.

Combine the rest of the ingredients, <u>except</u> the green chile, and beat until well-mixed. Stir in the crumbled bacon and green chile. Remove the hot skillet from the oven and pour in the corn bread mixture. Return to the oven and bake for 30 minutes or until nicely browned on top.

Serves 6.

Orange Breakfast Biscuits

Oranges and Christmas in Arizona have always seemed synonymous to me and I use a lot of this wonderful citrus fruit in all of my holiday cooking.

2 cups ALL-PURPOSE FLOUR
3 tsp. BAKING POWDER
1/2 tsp. SALT
1/4 cup SOLID VEGETABLE SHORTENING
3/4 cup MILK
1/4 cup SUGAR
1/2 tsp. ground CINNAMON
1/4 cup BUTTER, melted
1/2 cup ORANGE JUICE
1/2 cup SUGAR
2 Tbsp. GRATED ORANGE PEEL

Mix together the flour, baking powder, and salt and then, using a pastry cutter, cut the shortening into it until it is the size of small peas. Add the milk and stir into the dough with a fork. Shape into a ball and place on a lightly floured board or marble slab. Roll out to 1/4" inch thick rectangle. Mix together the 1/4 cup sugar and cinnamon and sprinkle over the dough. Roll the dough up, jelly roll style. Slice into 1-inch-thick rounds.

Mix together the butter, orange juice, sugar and orange peel and spread in the bottom of 10 x 14 inch cake pan. Place the biscuit dough, cut side down, on top of the orange and sugar mixture and bake in a 350 degree oven for 15 minutes or until biscuits are lightly browned and done. Turn upside down immediately so the topping will be on the top of the biscuits.

Makes 12 - 14 biscuits.

Applesauce Bread

Nothing is nicer than a sweet bread served to unexpected guests who drop in over the holiday for a cup of coffee.

2 cups APPLESAUCE
4 EGGS
3 cups SUGAR
1 Tbsp. GROUND CINNAMON
1 tsp. grated ORANGE PEEL
1/2 tsp. GROUND ALLSPICE
1 cup BUTTER or MARGARINE
1/2 cup APPLE JUICE
1/2 tsp. SALT
2 tsp. VANILLA
4 cups ALL-PURPOSE FLOUR
2 tsp. BAKING SODA

Mix the applesauce, eggs, sugar, cinnamon, orange peel, allspice, butter, apple juice, salt, and vanilla together in a food processor using a plastic blade. Put the flour and baking soda into a large mixing bowl. Stir in the applesauce mixture and mix well. Pour batter into 3 greased and floured 9 x 5 x 3 inch loaf pans. Bake in a 350 degree oven for 1 hour or until a toothpick inserted in the center comes out clean.

Makes 3 loaves.

Squash Muffins

Preheat oven to 375 degrees.

1 large EGG
1 cup MILK
3/4 cup cooked YELLOW SQUASH (such as Hubbard)
1/3 cup MARGARINE (room temperature)
1/2 cup SUGAR
1 tsp. grated ORANGE PEEL
2 1/4 cups all-purpose FLOUR
3 1/2 tsp. BAKING POWDER
1/2 tsp. SALT
1/4 cup GOLDEN RAISINS

Put egg and milk into a food processor with a plastic blade and blend. Add squash, margarine , sugar, orange peel and blend. Mix together flour, baking powder and salt in a separate bowl. Pour liquid ingredients from processor into bowl and blend until well mixed. Gently stir in raisins. Fill lightly greased or paper muffin cups 3/4 full and bake in a 375 degree oven for 20 - 25 minutes.

Makes approximately 12 muffins.

The following article in the *Arizona Daily Star* on December 22, 1912 advised parents about the type of toy that was best to buy their children for Christmas.

BEST TOYS FOR CHRISTMAS
They Should Suggest Action and Set
the Mind of the Child at Work.

In selecting toys for the children's Christmas, remember they should be such as to suggest action, and bring the imagination into play, as it is the child who plays, not the toy, and imagination is the soul of the play. The best toys are those which settle mind to work, and give the little brain scope for expansion. The wonderful mechanical toys sold in the shops are complete in themselves, and leave the child nothing to do but to wind them up and start them going. In this case, it is the toy that plays, not the child. Children soon weary of having nothing to do, and, losing interest in the monotonous repetitions, the little inquisitive mind sets about investigating the internal mechanism, greatly to the damage of the toy, which is soon ruined, and thrown away, while the child turns for amusement to the old toys that are so hopelessly undone that everything they are supposed to do must come from the play spirit in the child.

Strawberry, Prune, Almond Bread

This is one of those recipes that just "happened" one Christmas morning when we made a late decision for a bread for breakfast and just used what was in the cupboard.

Preheat oven to 350 degrees

1 cup WATER
1 cup STRAWBERRIES, cut in half
1 cup PITTED PRUNES
4 EGGS
3 cups SUGAR
1 cup MARGARINE, melted
1 tsp. ground CINNAMON
1 tsp. ground NUTMEG
1 tsp. grated ORANGE PEEL
1 cup SLIVERED ALMONDS
3 1/2 cups ALL-PURPOSE FLOUR
1 tsp. BAKING POWDER
2 tsp. BAKING SODA
1/2 tsp. SALT

Put water into blender, add strawberries and prunes, a little at a time, until fruit is chopped. You should have two cups. Add more strawberries and prunes, if needed, to make two cups. Put the eggs, sugar, melted margarine, cinnamon, nutmeg and orange peel into a food processor with a plastic blade and blend until well beaten. Add strawberry, prune mixture and the almonds and blend.

Put the flour, baking powder, baking soda and salt into a large mixing bowl, mix in the strawberry mixture and blend.

Spoon mixture into 3 lightly greased loaf pans and bake at 350 degrees for 30 minutes or until a toothpick inserted in the center comes out clean.

Makes 3 loaves.

Holiday Pan Dulce

This is a favorite traditional Mexican sweet bread that is served in many Arizona homes during the Holiday Season.

Preheat oven to 350 degrees

1/4 cup BOURBON
1 cup RAISINS
1 pkg. granulated YEAST
1/4 cup LUKEWARM MILK
1 Tbsp. SUGAR
1/2 tsp. SALT
1/4 lb. BUTTER, at room
    temperature

1/2 cup SUGAR
2 EGGS, lightly beaten
2 cups ALL-PURPOSE FLOUR
1 Tbsp. GRATED ORANGE PEEL
1 Tbsp. VANILLA
2 Tbsp. BLANCHED ALMONDS
POWDERED SUGAR

Pour the bourbon over the raisins in a saucepan and warm them. Then let them sit for 1 hour. Dissolve the yeast in the milk. Add the 1 tablespoon of sugar and the salt. Cream the butter and the 1/2 cup of sugar together. Stir in the yeast and milk mixture, then eggs, then flour and beat until the mixture is a smooth dough. Add the orange peel, vanilla and raisins and stir.

Grease and flour a 10-inch ring mold. Sprinkle almonds over the bottom of the pan. Gently spoon the dough over the almonds, cover with a towel and let sit in a warm place for 1 1/2 hours or until the dough has risen to the top of the mold.

Bake in a 350 degree oven for 35 - 40 minutes or until a light golden brown. Turn out on a rack to cool, dust with powdered sugar and serve.

Makes 1 ring loaf.

Lemon Bread

Preheat oven to 325 degrees.

1 cup SUGAR
6 Tbsp. MARGARINE, at room temperature
2 EGGS
1/4 cup LEMON JUICE
1 Tbsp. grated LEMON PEEL or ORANGE PEEL
1/2 cup MILK
1 1/2 cups ALL-PURPOSE FLOUR
1/2 tsp. SALT
1 tsp. BAKING POWDER
3/4 cup CHOPPED WALNUTS or PECANS

Mix the sugar, margarine, eggs, lemon juice, lemon peel and milk together. Stir in the flour, salt and baking powder and mix until smooth. Add the walnuts and spoon into a greased and floured 9 x 5 x 3 glass baking dish. Bake in a 325 degree oven for 50 minutes to 1 hour or until a toothpick inserted in the center comes out clean.

Makes 1 loaf.

Date Nut Bread

Preheat oven to 350 degrees.

1 cup SUGAR
1/4 cup BUTTER or
    MARGARINE
3/4 cup HOT WATER
1 EGG
1 tsp. BAKING SODA

1 3/4 cups ALL-PURPOSE FLOUR
1/2 tsp. SALT
1/4 tsp. ground NUTMEG
1 cup DATES, cut into pieces
1 cup WALNUTS, chopped

Mix the sugar, butter, water and egg into a food processor with a plastic blade. Put the baking soda, flour, salt and nutmeg into a large bowl, stir in the liquid mixture and beat until smooth. Stir in the dates and walnuts and spoon into a greased and floured 9 x 5 x 3 inch loaf pan. Bake in a 350 degree oven for 45 minutes or until a toothpick inserted in the center comes out clean.

Makes 1 loaf.

Buñuelos

In Mexican households it wouldn't be Christmas without this fritter served with sugar or a sweet such as jam or chocolate. This is the Arizona version.

3 cups ALL-PURPOSE FLOUR
1/2 tsp. SALT
1 tsp. BAKING POWDER
4 EGGS, lightly beaten
1/2 cup SOLID SHORTENING
1 oz BRANDY
WATER
MELTED BUTTER

Mix together the flour, salt and baking powder, stir in the eggs, shortening and brandy to make a soft dough (add water if necessary). Knead the dough on a lightly floured pastry board until it no longer sticks to the board. Brush the top of the dough with melted butter and let stand for an hour.

Then pinch off pieces approximately the size of a walnut. Roll them into long narrow strips and fry in deep fat until lightly browned. Serve with powdered sugar, syrup, or preserves, or dip into melted chocolate.

Lemon Muffins

Not only do lemons grow well outside in parts of Arizona, but I've even had good luck growing them inside my home in a room with lots of light.

Preheat oven to 375 degrees.

4 EGG YOLKS
1 cup MARGARINE at room temperature
1 cup SUGAR
1/2 cup LEMON JUICE
2 cups ALL-PURPOSE FLOUR
2 tsp. BAKING POWDER
1/2 tsp. SALT
1 Tbsp. grated LEMON RIND
4 EGG WHITES, stiffly beaten

Beat together the egg yolks, margarine, sugar and lemon juice in a food processor using a plastic blade. Put the flour, baking powder, salt and lemon rind into a large mixing bowl. Beat in the liquid ingredients, then fold in the egg whites. Fill lightly greased muffin tins to 3/4 full and bake in 375 degree oven for 20 minutes or until muffins test done when a toothpick inserted in the center of one comes out clean.

Makes approximately 2 dozen muffins.

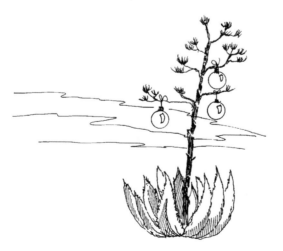

Holiday Coffee Cake

The sour cream in this recipe makes the texture of this coffee cake very light and moist. Perfect for drop-in guests or a great treat for Christmas breakfast.

Preheat oven to 350 degrees.

1/2 cup BUTTER, at room temperature
1 cup SUGAR
2 EGGS
1 cup SOUR CREAM
2 tsp. VANILLA
1 1/2 cups ALL-PURPOSE FLOUR
1 Tbsp. BAKING POWDER
1 tsp. BAKING SODA
1/2 cup PECANS, chopped
1/2 cup SUGAR
2 tsp. ground CINNAMON

Blend butter, the first cup of sugar, eggs, sour cream and vanilla in a food processor with a plastic blade. Put the flour, baking powder and baking soda into a large mixing bowl, stir in the liquid ingredients and blend. Grease and flour an 8 x 8 inch pan and pour half of the batter into it.   Mix the pecans with the remaining sugar and cinnamon and sprinkle half of the mixture on top of the batter. Spoon the rest of the batter into the pan, top with the remaining pecan mixture and bake in a 350 degree oven for 30 minutes or until a toothpick inserted in the center comes out clean.

Makes approx. 12 servings.

Pumpkin Bread

This bread makes a delightful addition to a holiday buffet or serve it with tea or cocoa on a blustery winter afternoon.

Preheat oven to 350 degrees.

1 cup BUTTER or MARGARINE, melted
2 cups CANNED PUMPKIN
4 EGGS, lightly beaten
3 cups SUGAR
2 tsp. BAKING SODA
1/2 tsp. BAKING POWDER
2 tsp. ground CINNAMON
1 tsp. ground NUTMEG
1 tsp. ground GINGER
1/2 tsp. ground CLOVES
1/2 tsp. SALT
3 1/2 cups ALL-PURPOSE FLOUR
1 cup PECANS

Blend the butter, pumpkin, eggs and sugar in a food processor until smooth. Put the baking soda, baking powder, cinnamon, nutmeg, ginger, cloves, salt and flour into a large mixing bowl. Stir in the pumpkin mixture, then stir into the pecans and spoon into three greased and floured loaf pans. Bake in a 350 degree oven for 30 minutes or until a toothpick inserted in the center comes out clean.

Makes 3 loaves.

Grandma's Gingerbread

President Taft had just signed the proclamation making Arizona the 48th state when "Grandma" Banes arrived. A long-time friend of my family, she described herself as "a fine figure of a woman and fit for anything." She was also an excellent cook and made this gingerbread on a wood stove until she was in her nineties.

Preheat oven to 350 degrees.

1/3 cup BUTTER or MARGARINE	**1 tsp. BAKING SODA**
1/2 cup SUGAR	**2 tsp. ground GINGER**
1 EGG	**1 tsp. ground CINNAMON**
1/2 cup MOLASSES	**1/2 tsp. ground CLOVES**
1 cup BUTTERMILK	**1 tsp. grated ORANGE PEEL**
2 cups ALL-PURPOSE FLOUR	**1/2 tsp. SALT**
2 tsp. BAKING POWDER	

Beat the butter, sugar, egg, molasses and buttermilk together in a food processor. Put the rest of the ingredients into a large mixing bowl. Stir in the liquid ingredients and spoon into an 8x8x2 inch lightly greased and floured baking pan. Bake in a 350 degree oven for 45 minutes or until bread tests done when a toothpick inserted in the center comes out clean. Best served warm with whipped cream.

Cranberry Bread

Preheat oven to 350 degrees.

1 cup BUTTER or MARGARINE, melted
1 can CRUSHED CRANBERRY SAUCE
4 EGGS, lightly beaten
3 cups SUGAR
2 tsp. BAKING SODA
1/2 tsp. BAKING POWDER
2 tsp. ground CINNAMON
1 tsp. ground NUTMEG
1 tsp. grated ORANGE PEEL
1/2 tsp. SALT
3 1/2 cups ALL-PURPOSE FLOUR
1 cup PECANS

Blend the butter, cranberry sauce, eggs and sugar in a food processor until smooth. Put the baking soda, baking powder, cinnamon, nutmeg, orange peel, salt and flour into a large mixing bowl. Stir in the cranberry mixture, then stir in the pecans and spoon into 3 greased and floured 9x5x3 inch loaf pans and bake in a 350 degree oven for 30 minutes or until a toothpick inserted in the center comes out clean.

Makes 3 loaves.

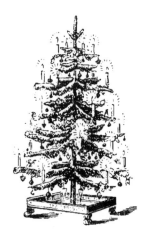

CHAPTER SIX

The Many Cultures of Arizona

Although the Indian heritage and the Mexican and Spanish influence upon Arizona is unmistakable and comes instantly to mind when speaking about Christmas in the Old Pueblo, the Valley of the Sun, and other places around the state, many other ethnic groups have also contributed greatly to way the people of Arizona celebrate Christmas.

The German immigrants who homesteaded in the Phoenix area brought their love of Christmas along with treasured family Christmas tree ornaments and the folk lore surrounding Kriss Kringle. They also introduced their famous sweet and sour recipes to the holiday feasting.

Spaniards and Basques helped settled the Flagstaff area. Many of them raised sheep and introduced to the area new and different ways of preparing lamb and mutton.

Southern gentlefolk settling in the new territory acquainted their neighbors with such customs as Buche Noels, Eggnog, and Rum Punch.

New Englanders brought with them their Protestant work ethic along with such Christmas customs as the Wassail bowl, cranberries used in all manner of ways, popcorn decorations, and the stern dictum that children had to be good all year in order for Santa Claus to visit them on Christmas Eve.

In the Thirties many of the families that headed for California to escape the "dust bowl" only got as far as Arizona after running out of money or stamina. They invested their fierce desire to work in the state and brought with them the Christmas customs inherited from their European ancestors.

Over the years, men chasing their dream of "gold in them thar hills," young men heeding the cry "go west young man, go west," and all who followed, have left their individual stamp on the way Christmas is celebrated in Arizona.

The customs and traditions of people from other parts of this country and other parts of the world, coupled with the Indian and Mexican influences make Christmas in Arizona one of the most wonderful, unique and joyful experiences in the world.

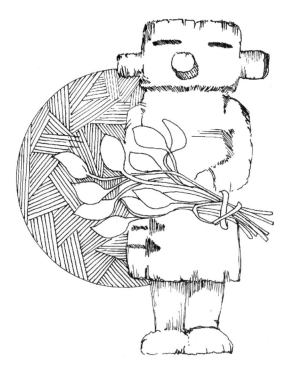

PHOTO FROM ARIZONA HISTORICAL SOCIETY LIBRARY

Christmas pageant at Villa Carondolet
1938 (St. Joseph's school)

PHOTO FROM ARIZONA HISTORICAL SOCIETY LIBRARY

Las Posadas—Christmas in Mexican Tradition - 1943

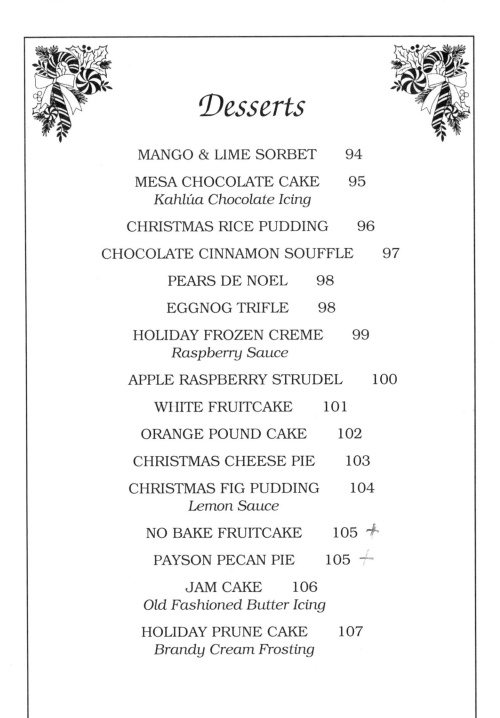

Desserts

MANGO & LIME SORBET   94

MESA CHOCOLATE CAKE   95
Kahlúa Chocolate Icing

CHRISTMAS RICE PUDDING   96

CHOCOLATE CINNAMON SOUFFLE   97

PEARS DE NOEL   98

EGGNOG TRIFLE   98

HOLIDAY FROZEN CREME   99
Raspberry Sauce

APPLE RASPBERRY STRUDEL   100

WHITE FRUITCAKE   101

ORANGE POUND CAKE   102

CHRISTMAS CHEESE PIE   103

CHRISTMAS FIG PUDDING   104
Lemon Sauce

NO BAKE FRUITCAKE   105

PAYSON PECAN PIE   105

JAM CAKE   106
Old Fashioned Butter Icing

HOLIDAY PRUNE CAKE   107
Brandy Cream Frosting

Mango & Lime Sorbet

This makes a light finale or use between courses of a large holiday meal to "refresh the palate."

1 cup WATER
1/2 cup SUGAR
1 1/2 cup MANGOES, peeled and chopped
     (Best bet is the fresh peeled mangoes in the
     refrigerated section of your produce department.)
JUICE of 2 LIMES
1/2 tsp. GRATED ORANGE PEEL
LIME PEEL

Stir the water and sugar together in a saucepan and cook over medium heat for 5 minutes, stirring occasionally. Let cool to room temperature. Puree the mangoes and lime juice in a blender until smooth. Stir the mango mixture into the sugar water. Stir in the grated orange peel and freeze until set up. Garnish with twisted lime peel.

Serves 4.

Mesa Chocolate Cake

This cake is a splurge, but is very moist and makes an extra special treat for the holidays.

Preheat oven to 350 degrees.

1 cup **MARGARINE**
3/4 cup **COCOA**
1 cup **HOT WATER**
2 cups **SUGAR or FRUCTOSE**
2 large **EGGS or 3 medium size EGGS**
2 tsp. **VANILLA**
3 Tbsp. **KAHLÚA**®
2 cups **ALL-PURPOSE FLOUR**
1 cup **SOUR CREAM**
1/2 tsp. **SALT**
1 tsp. **BAKING SODA**

Put the margarine, cocoa and hot water into a microwave safe bowl. Cook in the microwave on high for 1 minute or until the margarine has melted, stirring once in the cooking process. Cream the sugar and eggs together in a food processor or mixer. Add vanilla and Kahlúa® and blend again.

After chocolate mixture has cooled, pour into egg mixture and blend. Mix together the flour, salt and baking soda in a large bowl and fold in the cooled chocolate mixture just until blended. Stir in sour cream. <u>Do not overbeat</u>. Pour batter into a 9 x 13 inch lightly greased and floured pan. Bake in a 350 degree oven for 30 minutes or until toothpick inserted in center of cake comes out clean.

Kahlúa® Chocolate Icing

1 1/2 cups **SUGAR or FRUCTOSE**
1/4 lb. **MARGARINE, melt in microwave**
6 Tbsp. **MILK**
3 Tbsp. **KAHÚLA**®
2 tsp. **ORANGE PEEL**
1 cup **WALNUTS, CHOPPED**
1/2 cup **COCOA**

Mix in food processor to make a smooth icing.

Christmas Rice Pudding

Wagon trains brought such precious commodities into the Arizona territory in the 1800's as rice, sugar and raisins. Territorial housewives used these ingredients sparingly except at Christmas.

Preheat oven to 350 degrees.

1/2 cup SUGAR
1/2 tsp. SALT
1 tsp. VANILLA
3 EGGS, lightly beaten
3 cups MILK
3/4 cup COOKED WHITE RICE
1/2 tsp. ground NUTMEG
1/2 cup RAISINS

Beat the sugar, salt and vanilla into the eggs. Stir in the milk. Then stir in the rice, nutmeg and raisins. Spoon into a greased baking dish and set in a shallow pan of water, making sure the water does not come more than halfway up the sides of the dish. Bake in a 350 degree oven for 30 minutes. Serve warm with vanilla ice cream or whipped cream.

Serves 6.

From an Arizona resident to the ***Arizona Daily Star***, December 24, 1890

CHRISTMAS FIG PUDDING

Materials - Beef suet, 1/2 pound; flour, 3 cups; figs, 1 pound; brown sugar, 1 cup; candied orange peel, 2 tablespoons; salt, 3 teaspoonfuls; cloves, 1/8 teaspoonful; grated nutmeg, 1/2 teaspoonful; cinnamon, 1/2 teaspoonful; eggs, 2; sweet milk, 1/2 cup.

Utensils - Mold, teaspoon, food chopper, sieve and egg beater.

Directions - Chop the suet fine and mix with one cup of the flour; then add the figs chopped fine, brown sugar, rolled smooth, and the orange peel chopped fine and simmered in a little water or syrup. Mix all together thoroughly. Pass all the remaining ingredients through a sieve, then sift again into the first mixture and mix thoroughly. Beat the eggs, add the milk and stir into the dry ingredients to form a stiff dough. Turn into the mold well buttered and steam six hours. Serve with hard sauce. If this is put into a covered mold and set in boiling water in the fireless cooker, thirty minutes on the fire will answer and finish in the cooker.

Chocolate Cinnamon Souffle

Preheat oven to 400 degrees.

3 Tbsp. BUTTER
3 Tbsp. ALL-PURPOSE FLOUR
1 cup MILK
2 squares SEMI-SWEET CHOCOLATE, melted
3 Tbsp. BRANDY
1 cup SUGAR
1/4 tsp. SALT
1 tsp. ground CINNAMON, divided
6 EGG YOLKS, lightly beaten
6 EGG WHITES
1/2 tsp. CREAM OF TARTAR
POWDERED SUGAR

Let the butter melt in a heavy saucepan. Whisk in the flour to make a roux. Stir in the milk and whisk for two minutes. Mix the brandy into the melted chocolate and then stir into the milk and flour mixture. Add the salt, sugar and 1/2 teaspoon cinnamon and cook, whisking constantly, until sauce thickens and is smooth. Remove from heat and let cool. Beat in the egg yolks.

Beat the egg whites until they start to stiffen. Add the cream of tartar and continue beating until stiff. Fold into the chocolate mixture and pour into a 6-cup souffle dish that has been lightly buttered and dusted with sugar. Set the souffle dish into a pan of hot water and bake for 5 minutes in a 400 degree oven. Reduce the heat to 350 degrees and bake for 30 minutes longer or until done. Mix the powdered sugar with the remaining cinnamon and dust the top of the souffle. Serve at once.

Serves 4 - 6.

Pears de Noel

2 cups DRY RED WINE
1 cup WATER
3/4 cup SUGAR
6 WHOLE CLOVES
1 CINNAMON STICK,
   broken in half

1 Tbsp. grated ORANGE PEEL
1 Tbsp. VANILLA
6 large firm PEARS
prepared CHOCOLATE SYRUP
1 Tbsp. ORANGE FLAVORED LIQUEUR
MINT LEAVES

Cook the wine, water, sugar, cloves, cinnamon stick, orange peel and vanilla over medium-high heat for 10 minutes in a large saucepan. While this is cooking, peel the pears, leaving the stem on. Place the pears in the wine mixture, reduce the heat to simmer and poach the pears for 10 minutes. Remove the pan from the heat and let the pears cool to room temperature in the syrup. Remove the pears from the syrup and chill in the refrigerator for at least an hour.

Mix the chocolate syrup with the orange liqueur and spoon onto dessert plates. Place a pear on top of the chocolate, garnish with mint leaves and serve.

Serves 6.

Eggnog Trifle

16 LADYFINGERS, split in half lengthwise
2 ENVELOPES UNFLAVORED GELATIN
1/2 cup COLD WATER
1 qt. EGGNOG
1 Tbsp. WHITE RUM
WHIPPED CREAM
RUM
STRAWBERRIES
SLICED KIWI

Line the bottom and sides of a 9 inch spring form pan with the lady finger halves. Dissolve the gelatin in the cold water and then stir into the eggnog. Stir in rum and chill in refrigerator until almost set, then spoon into the ladyfinger shell. Chill until set. Remove sides of spring form pan and garnish with whipped cream laced with rum. Top with sliced strawberries and sliced kiwi.

Serves 8 - 10.

Holiday Frozen Creme

1 cup WHIPPING CREAM
2 tsp. SUGAR
1 qt. FRENCH VANILLA ICE CREAM
1/4 cup GREEN CREME DE MENTHE
1/2 cup PECANS, chopped
RASPBERRY SAUCE

Beat the cream until it starts to stiffen. Add the sugar and continue beating until it forms peaks. Beat the ice cream until soft, then fold into the whipped cream. Gently stir in the creme de menthe and pecans and spoon into a bowl. Cover with plastic wrap and freeze, stirring twice during the freezing process. Pour Raspberry Sauce into the bottom of a dessert plate, place a scoop of the frozen dessert on top of the sauce and serve.

Serves 4 - 6

Raspberry Sauce

1 cup ripe RED RASPBERRIES, fresh or frozen
3/4 cup SUGAR or FRUCTOSE
3/4 cup WHITE WINE
1 tsp. grated ORANGE PEEL

Combine all the ingredients in a saucepan and bring to a boil, stirring occasionally and mashing the berries. When the sugar has completely dissolved, let cool. Then strain into a jar and chill in the refrigerator for at least 2 hours before serving.

Makes approximately 2 cups.

Apple Raspberry Strudel

Preheat oven to 375 degrees.

1 sheet PUFF PASTRY	1/4 tsp. SALT
2 large-sized TART APPLES, peeled, cored and sliced	1/2 tsp. ground ORANGE PEEL
	1/4 cup SLICED ALMONDS
1/4 cup fresh RASPBERRIES fresh or frozen	2 Tbsp. ALMOND FLAVORED LIQUEUR
1/4 cup SUGAR	1 EGG
1/2 tsp. ground CINNAMON	WATER
1/4 tsp. ground NUTMEG	

Place the dough in the center of a non-stick cookie sheet and layer the apples down the center of the pastry the long way. Place the raspberries on top of the apples, sprinkle with the sugar, cinnamon, nutmeg, salt, orange peel and almonds. Pour the liqueur over the fruit. Pick one third of the pastry up and place over the apples, then lift the other 1/3 up and lap over the first.

Lightly beat the egg. Add just a drop of cold water and, using a pastry brush, brush the egg onto the top and sides of the dough. Bake in a 375 degree oven for 20 minutes or until the dough is nicely browned. Slice and serve either warm or with a small scoop of vanilla ice cream on the side.

Serves 4 - 6.

White Fruitcake

Some like their fruitcake dark, some like it light. There are also those who claim not to like fruitcake at all . . . this one will change their minds!

Preheat oven to 250 degrees.

2 lb. WHITE RAISINS
1 cup WHITE RUM
1 lb. CANDIED CHERRIES, chopped
1 lb. CANDIED PINEAPPLE, chopped
1/2 lb. PRESERVED CITRON, chopped
1/4 lb. LEMON PEEL, chopped
1/4 lb. ORANGE PEEL, chopped
4 1/2 cups CAKE FLOUR
2 cups BUTTER or MARGARINE
2 1/4 cups SUGAR
8 - 10 EGGS, lightly beaten
1 tsp. BAKING POWDER
1/2 tsp. SALT
1 cup ORANGE JUICE
1 cup ALMONDS, blanched and slivered
1 cup COCONUT, grated
RUM to soak cake

Stir raisins into rum and let stand overnight. Mix candied fruit with 1 1/2 cups flour. Cream butter and sugar together; add eggs and mix well. Add remaining 3 cups flour, baking powder, salt and beat well. Stir in orange juice, raisins, floured fruit, almonds and coconut. Mix the batter well and then pour into 2 well greased 9" tube pans or 4 greased paper-lined 9" x 5" x 3" loaf pans. Bake in a 250 degree oven for 2 1/2 hours. Cool for 30 minutes before removing from the pans. Soak with rum, wrap in clean tea towels, then aluminum foil and store in refrigerator until ready to use.

Makes 2 tube cakes or 4 loaves.

Orange Pound Cake

I know, I know! All that butter and all those eggs! But it's oh so good for a special holiday treat. Great served with chocolate flavored coffee. You can go on your diet after New Year's!

Preheat oven to 350 degrees.

3 cups SUGAR
1 cup BUTTER
6 EGGS, lightly beaten
1/2 tsp. BAKING SODA
1/2 tsp. SALT
1 cup BUTTERMILK
3 cups ALL-PURPOSE FLOUR
1/2 cup FRESH ORANGE JUICE
1/4 cup ORANGE FLAVORED LIQUEUR
1/4 cup POWDERED SUGAR

Cream together the sugar and butter. Stir in the eggs, soda and salt, then the buttermilk and flour and beat until smooth. Spoon into a lightly greased and floured bundt pan and bake in a 350 degree oven for 1 hour or until a toothpick inserted in cake comes out clean.

Mix together the orange juice and liqueur and drizzle over the warm cake. Dust with the powdered sugar, let cool and serve.

Christmas Cheese Pie

This is our version of a favorite holiday dessert among the many Italian-American families living in Arizona.

Preheat oven to 350 degrees.

3 cups (1 1/2 lbs.) RICOTTA CHEESE
1/4 cup ALL-PURPOSE FLOUR
2 Tbsp. grated ORANGE RIND
1 Tbsp. grated LEMON PEEL
1 Tbsp. WHITE VANILLA
1/2 tsp. SALT
1/4 tsp. ground NUTMEG
4 EGGS, lightly beaten
1 cup SUGAR
9 inch DEEP DISH PIE CRUST
KIWI SLICES
POWDERED SUGAR

Mix all the ingredients together, <u>except</u> the kiwi and powdered sugar, and spoon into pie shell. Bake in a 350 degree oven for 45 minutes or until firm in the center. Let cool on a rack and then dust with powdered sugar. Garnish with sliced kiwi and serve.

Serves 6 - 8.

Christmas Fig Pudding

*We bought a house in Tucson one afternoon after much delibera-
tion, but the fact that there was a fig tree in the back yard was what
finally made us decide to go ahead.*

Preheat oven to 350 degrees.

3/4 cup BUTTER
1 cup SUGAR
3 EGGS
3/4 cup DRIED FIGS
1/2 cup MILK
1 tsp. VANILLA
2 cups ALL-PURPOSE FLOUR
1 tsp. BAKING SODA
1/2 tsp. ground NUTMEG
1 tsp. ground CINNAMON
1/2 tsp. SALT

Put the butter, sugar, eggs, figs, milk and vanilla in a food
processor and blend. Put the flour, baking soda, nutmeg, cinnamon and salt in a large mixing bowl. Stir in the fig mixture and
blend well. Spoon into a pudding mold or bowl, place in a pan of
water. Make sure that the water does not come up more than halfway up the sides of the mold. Bake in a 350 degree oven for 45
minutes or until pudding is set. Serve warm with Lemon Sauce.

Serves 6 - 8.

Lemon Sauce

1/2 cup SUGAR
3 Tbsp. ALL-PURPOSE FLOUR
3 EGG YOLKS, lightly beaten
3/4 cup WATER
3/4 cup LEMON JUICE
1 Tbsp. BUTTER
1 tsp. grated LEMON PEEL

Mix all the ingredients together into the top of a double boiler
and cook, stirring constantly, until the sauce is smooth and slightly
thickened. Serve hot or cold over Christmas Fig Pudding.

No-Bake Fruitcake

1 **cup SEEDLESS GOLDEN RAISINS**
2 **Tbsp. BRANDY**
4 **cups GRAHAM CRACKER CRUMBS**
1/3 **cup GREEN CANDIED FRUIT**
1/3 **cup RED CANDIED FRUIT**
1/3 **cup YELLOW CANDIED FRUIT**
1 **cup PITTED DATES, chopped**
1 **cup PECANS, chopped**
1 **cup MINIATURE MARSHMALLOWS**
1 **can (14 oz.) SWEETENED CONDENSED MILK**

Put the raisins and the brandy into a saucepan and heat until warm. Remove from the heat and let stand for 10 minutes. Line a 9 by 5 inch loaf pan with waxed paper. Mix all the ingredients together, until the crumbs are thoroughly moistened. Pack securely into the pan and cover tightly. Chill at least two days before slicing. Slice thinly and serve.

Makes a 2 1/4-pound loaf.

Payson Pecan Pie

A concert pianist of our acquaintance had a home in Phoenix and a hideaway in Payson. We'd receive a phone call every year right after Thanksgiving reminding us that this pecan pie would be the best Christmas card he could receive.

Preheat oven to 400 degrees.

3 **EGGS, lightly beaten**
1/2 **cup SUGAR**
1/2 **tsp. SALT**
1 **cup LIGHT CORN SYRUP**
2 **tsp. VANILLA**

1 **Tbsp. BOURBON**
1 **cup PECANS, chopped**
9 **inch PIE SHELL**
PECAN HALVES

Mix the eggs, sugar, salt, corn syrup, vanilla, bourbon and chopped pecans together. Pour into pie shell and layer the pecan halves on top of the filling. Bake in a 400 degree oven for 10 minutes, then reduce heat to 325 degrees and cook for 30 more minutes. Let cool and serve with whipped cream.

Serves 6.

Jam Cake

Preheat oven to 325 degrees.

3 EGGS
1/2 cup BUTTER or MARGARINE, at room temperature
1 cup SUGAR
1 tsp. VANILLA
1/2 cup BUTTERMILK
1 cup RASPBERRY PRESERVES
1/2 cup STRAWBERRY PRESERVES
1 1/2 cups ALL-PURPOSE FLOUR
1/2 tsp. ground ALLSPICE
1/2 tsp. ground CINNAMON
1/2 tsp. ground CLOVES
1 tsp. BAKING SODA
1/2 tsp. SALT
1/2 cup RAISINS
1 cup PECANS, chopped

Put eggs in food processor and beat. Then add butter, sugar and vanilla and beat. Add the buttermilk and preserves and beat again. In a large mixing bowl mix together the flour, allspice, cinnamon, cloves, baking soda and salt. Combine the liquid ingredients with dry ingredients and mix well. Stir in raisins and pecans. Lightly grease and flour two 8 inch square cake pans. Pour in the batter and bake for 45 - 50 minutes in a 325 degree oven or until it tests done when a toothpick inserted in the center comes out clean. Let cool on wire rack, dust with powdered sugar or ice with old-fashioned butter icing.

Old-Fashioned Butter Icing

3 cups POWDERED SUGAR
1/2 cup BUTTER or MARGARINE
3 Tbsp. MILK
1 Tbsp. VANILLA

Mix all the ingredients together. Add more milk if necessary to make it smooth and spreadable. Frost the Jam Cake.

Holiday Prune Cake

Even those folks not fond of prunes will like them when incorporated in this easy to make, old-fashioned cake!

Preheat oven to 325 degrees.

3 EGGS
1/2 cup VEGETABLE OIL
1 tsp. VANILLA
1 cup BUTTERMILK
2 cups ALL-PURPOSE FLOUR
2 tsp. BAKING POWDER
1 tsp. BAKING SODA
3/4 tsp. SALT
1 1/2 cups SUGAR
1/4 tsp. ground CARDAMON
1 tsp. grated ORANGE PEEL
1 tsp. ground CINNAMON
1 tsp. ground NUTMEG
1 Tbsp. BRANDY
1 cup PRUNES, cooked and chopped
1 cup PECANS, chopped

Beat the eggs, oil, vanilla, and buttermilk in a large mixing bowl. Stir in the flour, baking powder, baking soda, salt, sugar, cardamon, orange peel, cinnamon, nutmeg and brandy. Then add the prunes and pecans. Spoon into a 13 x 9 x 2 inch lightly greased and floured baking pan. Bake in a 325 degree oven for 35 to 40 minutes or until cake tests done when a toothpick inserted in the center comes out clean. Cool on a wire rack. Frost with Brandy Cream Frosting.

Brandy Cream Frosting

1/2 cup BUTTER or MARGARINE, at room temperature
1 lb. POWDERED SUGAR
1/4 cup BRANDY
2 Tbsp. MILK

Mix all the ingredients together until smooth enough to frost cake, adding more milk if necessary.

Cookies and Candies

Classic Wedding Cookies

My cousin, Sandy Thomas, has won several first place awards in Tucson for her baking. She is especially well known for creating great wedding cakes and delectibles.

Preheat oven to 300 degrees.

1 **stick (1/2 cup) MARGARINE, at room temperature**
2 **Tbsp. SUGAR**
2 **tsp. VANILLA**
1/4 **tsp. SALT**
1 **cup ALL-PURPOSE FLOUR**
1/2 **cup PECANS, chopped**
POWDERED SUGAR

Cream margarine and sugar together. Add vanilla and salt. Alternately mix in flour and pecans. Roll into small balls the size of a pecan. Place on a very lightly greased cookie sheet and put into a cold oven. Bake at 300 degrees for 15 minutes or until done. Roll in powdered sugar while still warm.

Yield: approximately 3 dozen cookies.

Lemon Drop Cookies

1/4 **cup MILK**
1 **cup SUGAR**
1 **tsp. ORANGE PEEL, grated**
2 **EGGS**
1 1/2 **Tbsp. LEMON JUICE**
1/2 **cup BUTTER or MARGARINE, at room temperature**
2 **cups ALL-PURPOSE FLOUR**
1 **tsp. BAKING POWDER**
1/4 **tsp. SALT**
1/2 **tsp. ground CARDAMON**
24 **PECAN HALVES**

Blend the milk, sugar, orange peel, eggs, lemon juice and butter in a food processor with a plastic blade or mixer. Add the flour, baking powder, salt and cardamon and blend until smooth. Drop by the teaspoonful onto a well-greased cookie sheet. Press a pecan half into the top of each cookie and bake at 375 degrees for 10 - 12 minutes or until done.

Yield: 24 cookies.

Mincemeat Peanut Butter Cookies

Preheat oven to 375 degrees.

2 EGGS
2/3 cup VEGETABLE SHORTENING
2 cups SUGAR
1 Tbsp. VANILLA
1/2 cup MILK
1 cup PEANUT BUTTER
1 1/2 cups MINCEMEAT
4 cups ALL-PURPOSE FLOUR
2 tsp. BAKING POWDER
1/2 tsp. SALT
1 tsp. grated ORANGE PEEL

Put eggs, shortening, sugar, vanilla, and milk into a food processor with a plastic blade and blend until light lemon yellow color. Add peanut butter and mincemeat and blend. Put flour, baking powder, salt and orange peel into a large mixing bowl. Pour the liquid mixture into the bowl and stir until well mixed. Form into small balls and place on a lightly greased cookie sheet. Bake at 375 degrees for 10 - 12 minutes.

Yield: 5 - 6 dozen cookies.

Almond Meringue Cookies

Preheat oven to 400 degrees.

2 cups SLIVERED ALMONDS
3/4 cup HONEY
1 tsp. WHITE VANILLA
2 EGG WHITES, stiffly beaten
2/3 cup SHREDDED COCONUT

Grind the almonds, a few at a time, in a food processor with a steel blade. Then blend the honey and vanilla into the almonds. Fold the egg whites into the almond mixture then shape into one-inch balls using a teaspoon. Roll in the coconut and place approximately two inches apart on a baking sheet sprayed with vegetable coating. Flatten the cookies and bake in a 400 degree oven for 8 to 10 minutes or until golden brown. Cool on a wire rack.

Yield: approximately 2 dozen cookies.

Kahlúa® Truffles

Truffles always sound so elegant and fancy but, in truth, they are extremely easy to make.

6 oz. SEMI-SWEET CHOCOLATE
1/2 cup WHIPPING CREAM
2 Tbsp. KAHLÚA®
3 Tbsp. BUTTER
2 Tbsp. POWDERED SUGAR
COCOA

Put the chocolate and cream into a bowl. Place in the microwave and melt, stirring occasionally. When the chocolate has melted, stir in the Kahlúa, butter and powdered sugar and beat until smooth. Let cool. Line a cookie sheet with wax paper and sprinkle cocoa over it. Drop the cooled chocolate mixture onto the cocoa with a teaspoon, and shape with fingers. Let stand for 1 hour before serving.

Yield: approximately 1 dozen truffles.

Chocolate Rum Balls

4 squares (4 oz.) SEMI-SWEET CHOCOLATE
3/4 cup WHIPPING CREAM
3/4 cup SUGAR
1 Tbsp. RUM
1 Tbsp. BUTTER
1/2 cup PECANS, coarsely ground

Heat the chocolate and cream in the microwave for 2 - 3 minutes or until the chocolate has melted. Stir in the sugar, rum and butter. Let cool in the refrigerator overnight, then shape into small balls and roll in the ground pecans.

Yield: approximately 48 balls.

Stuffed Dates

1 box PITTED DATES
1 cup ALMONDS
POWDERED SUGAR

Make a slit in one side of the dates with a sharp knife, insert an almond, roll the dates in the powdered sugar and serve.

Bourbon Balls

2 cups VANILLA WAFERS, finely crushed
2 cups POWDERED SUGAR
3 Tbsp. LIGHT CORN SYRUP
4 Tbsp. COCOA
1 cup PECANS, finely chopped
2 Tbsp. BOURBON
POWDERED SUGAR

Mix all the ingredients together, roll into approximately 1 inch balls, then roll in powdered sugar.

Yield: approximately 2 dozen balls.

Wickenburg Pralines

2 cups SUGAR
1 tsp. BAKING SODA
1/4 tsp. SALT
1 cup BUTTERMILK
2 Tbsp. BUTTER or MARGARINE
2 cups PECAN HALVES
1 tsp. VANILLA

Bring the sugar, soda, salt and buttermilk to a rolling boil in a saucepan. Stir in butter and pecans and boil until it reaches 230 degrees. Remove from the heat and stir in the vanilla. Let cool for 5 minutes then beat until mixture loses its sheen. Drop by the tablespoonful onto waxed paper.

Yield: approximately 2 dozen.

The following recipe was on the Society page of the December 20th 1914 issue of the **Arizona Daily Star**.

The Christmas Cake

An Original Recipe
by Jessamine Chapman Williams

One lb. butter
One lb. brown sugar
One lb. eggs (9 or 10)
One lb. flour (sifted)
One Tbsp. cinnamon
One nutmeg (grated)
Two tsp. mace

Two tsp. allspice
One tsp. clove
Two tsp. baking powder
One-half pint brandy
Two lbs. raisins
One lb. English currants
One lb. figs

One lb. Sultana raisins
One lb. citron
One lb. shelled almonds
1/2 preserved lemon rind
1/2 preserved orange rind
2-4 squares of chocolate

PREPARATION OF FRUIT —The raisins should be washed and cut in small pieces with a scissors. The English currants should be washed and dried. The figs, lemon and orange rinds are chopped finely. The citron is shaved in very thin slices, then cut in strips. The almonds should be blanched and shredded finely.

COMBINING THE INGREDIENTS—Cream the butter, add sugar gradually, beat thoroughly, separate yolks and whites of eggs. Beat yolks until thick and lemon colored and add to the butter and sugar. Add two-thirds of the flour sifted several times with the spices and baking powder. Mix the remaining third of flour with the mixture of fruits and nuts, reserving the citron; add fruit, melted chocolate, brandy, and, lastly, the whites of eggs beaten stiff and dry.

PREPARATION FOR BAKING—Line deep pans with several layers of paper, oiling the upper one. Spread one-half the batter in the pans, sprinkle the citron dredged with flour over the batter, and spread the remaining batter over it. Cover with oiled paper.

THE BAKING —Steaming is preferable to baking for there is less danger of burning. Either steam three hours and finish the cooking by baking one and one-half hours in a slow oven, or bake four hours in very slow oven. While the cake is still warm, pour over it one-half pint of sherry wine, then allow it to stand in tins until cold. It may then be filled with almond paste and covered with a plain frosting.

ALMOND PASTE FILLING—This filling is delicious and may be used on any cake of the kind. It is spread one or two inches thick on the cake before the frosting is put on.

One pound almond paste or blanched almonds ground to a powder. Three-quarters pound confectioner's sugar. Rose water to moisten.

Work the paste and sifted sugar together on a board or in a large bowl, using a fork or the fingers. Add rose water to make of a consistency to spread.

FROSTING—Cover the almond paste filling with a plain frosting made of confectioner's sugar, white of egg and flavoring. The cake can be frosted again with an ornamental frosting or any kind desired when ready to use.

Index

Meet
the
Author

Lynn Nusom has owned and operated award-winning restaurants and was the executive chef of a four-star four-diamond hotel. He writes a syndicated newspaper column on food, reviews cook books, writes magazine articles on cooking and makes frequent appearances on television demonstrating cooking techniques.

Lynn Nusom has written a wide variety of cook books including; *Cooking in the Land of Enchantment, Spoon Desserts; Custards, Cremes and Elegant Fruit Desserts, Christmas in Arizona, Billy the Kid Cook Book, Christmas in New Mexico,* the *New Mexico Cook Book* and *The Tequila Cook Book.* He is also featured in a series of video tapes on Southwestern cooking.

The author makes his home in southern New Mexico with his wife, Guylyn, where they operate a very successful catering service.

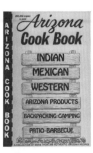

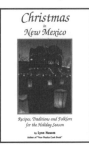
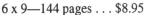

ORDER BLANK

GOLDEN WEST PUBLISHERS

☼ 4113 N. Longview Ave. • Phoenix, AZ 85014

602-265-4392 • **1-800-658-5830** • FAX 602-279-6901

Qty	Title	Price	Amount
	Apple Lovers's Cook Book	6.95	
	Arizona Cook Book	5.95	
	Arizona Small Game Recipes	5.95	
	Best Barbecue Recipes	5.95	
	Chili-Lovers' Cook Book	5.95	
	Chip and Dip Lovers Cook Book	5.95	
	Christmas in Arizona Cook Book	8.95	
	Christmas in New Mexico Cook Book	8.95	
	Citrus Lovers Cook Book	6.95	
	Cowboy Cartoon Cook Book	5.95	
	Date Recipes	6.95	
	Easy RV Recipes	6.95	
	Joy of Muffins	5.95	
	Mexican Family Favorites	6.95	
	New Mexico Cook Book	5.95	
	Pecan Lovers Cook Book	6.95	
	Quick-n-Easy Mexican Recipes	5.95	
	Salsa Lovers Cook Book	5.95	
	Tequila Cook Book	7.95	
	Wholly Frijoles! The Whole Bean Cook Book	6.95	
	Add $2.00 to total order for shipping & handling		**$2.00**

☐ My Check or Money Order Enclosed. . . . . $

☐ MasterCard ☐ VISA

(Payable in U.S. funds)

Acct. No.   Exp. Date

Signature

Name   Telephone

Address

City/State/Zip

Call or write for FREE catalog

11/95   MasterCard and VISA Orders Accepted ($20 Minimum)

X'mas AZ

This order blank may be photo-copied.